The GUITAR STRUMMER'S Christmas Songbook

PREFACE

This book is designed especially to get you playing (and singing!) along with your favorite Christmas songs. The songs are arranged in lead sheet format, giving you the chords, melody, and lyrics. Strum patterns are also written above the staff as an accompaniment suggestion. Strum the chords in the rhythm indicated. Use the chord diagrams found at the top of the first page of the arrangement for the appropriate chord voicings.

ISBN 0-634-04864-3

HAL•LEONARD®
CORPORATION

7777 W. BLUEMOUND RD. P.O. BOX 13819 MILWAUKEE, WI 53213

Visit Hal Leonard Online at
www.halleonard.com

The GUITAR STRUMMERS' Christmas Songbook

CONTENTS

All Through the Night

Welsh Folksong

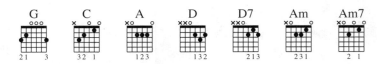

Verse

Moderately Slow

1. Sleep, my child, and peace at-tend thee, all through the night.
2., 3. *See Additional Lyrics*

Guard-ian an-gels God will send thee, all through the night.

Soft, the drow-sy hours are creep-ing, hill and vale in slum-ber sleep-ing.

God, his lov-ing vig-il keep-ing, all through the night. night.

Additional Lyrics

2. While the moon, her watch is keeping,
   All through the night.
   While the weary world is sleeping,
   All through the night.
   Through your dreams you're swiftly stealing,
   Visions of delight revealing,
   Christmas time is so appealing,
   All through the night.

3. You, my God, a babe of wonder,
   All through the night.
   Dreams you can't break from thunder,
   All through the night.
   Children's dreams cannot be broken,
   Life is but a lovely token.
   Christmas should be softly spoken,
   All through the night.

Almost Day

Words and Music by Huddie Ledbetter

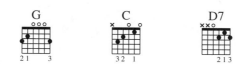

Verse

Moderate Square Dance

1. Chick-ens a-crowin' for mid-night, _ it's al-most day. Chick-ens a-crowin' for
2. *See Additional Lyrics*

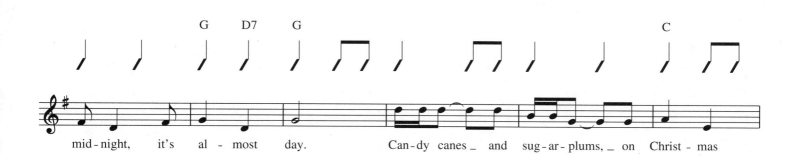

mid-night, it's al-most day. Can-dy canes _ and sug-ar-plums, _ on Christ-mas

Day. Can-dy canes _ and sug-ar-plums, _ on Christ-mas Day. Day.

Additional Lyrics

2. Mama'll stuff a turkey on Christmas Day.
   Mama'll stuff a turkey on Christmas Day.
   Santa Claus is coming on Christmas Day.
   Santa Claus is coming on Christmas Day.

Angels We Have Heard on High

Traditional French Carol
Translated by James Chadwick

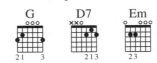

Additional Lyrics

2. Shepherds why this jubilee,
   Why your joyous strains prolong?
   What the gladsome tidings be
   Which inspire your heavenly song?

Ave Maria

By Franz Schubert

Verse
Reverently

1. A - ve Ma - ri - a! Gra - ti - a__ ple - na, Ma-
2. *See additional lyrics*

ri - a__ gra - ti - a ple - na, Ma - ri - a gra - ti - a__ ple - na, A -

cont. rhy. sim.

ve, _____ A - ve! Do - mi - nus, _____ Do - mi - nus__ te - cum, Be - ne -

dic - ta tu in mu - li - e - re - bus et be - ne - dic - tus, et

be - ne - dic - tus, fruc - tus ven - tris, ven - tris tu - i, Je - sus.

A - ve Ma - ri - a!

Additional Lyrics

2. Ave Maria!
Mater Dei, Ora pro nobis peccatoribus,
Ora ora pro nobis, Ora, ra pro nobis peccatoribus.
None et in hora mortis, in hora mortis nostrae,
In hora mortis, mortis nostrae,
In hora mortis nostrae.
Ave Maria!

Away in a Manger

Anonymous Text (vv. 1, 2)
Text by John T. McFarland (v. 3)
Music by Jonathan E. Spillman

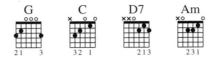

Verse

Sweetly

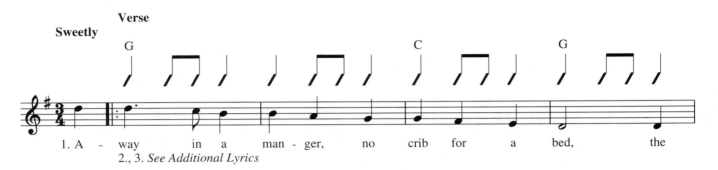

1. A - way in a man - ger, no crib for a bed, the
2., 3. *See Additional Lyrics*

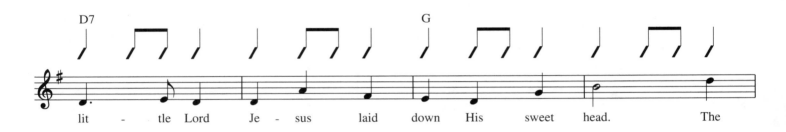

lit - tle Lord Je - sus laid down His sweet head. The

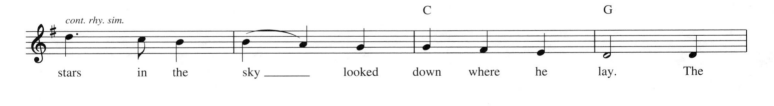

stars in the sky _____ looked down where he lay. The

lit - tle Lord Je - sus a - sleep on the hay. 2. The there.

Additional Lyrics

2. The cattle are lowing, the baby awakes,
   But little Lord Jesus, no crying He makes.
   I love Thee, Lord Jesus, look down from the sky
   And stay by my cradle 'til morning is nigh.

3. Be near me, Lord Jesus, I ask Thee to stay
   Close by me forever and love me I pray.
   Bless all the dear children in Thy tender care
   And take us to heaven to live with Thee there.

Bring a Torch, Jeannette, Isabella

17th Century French Provencal Carol

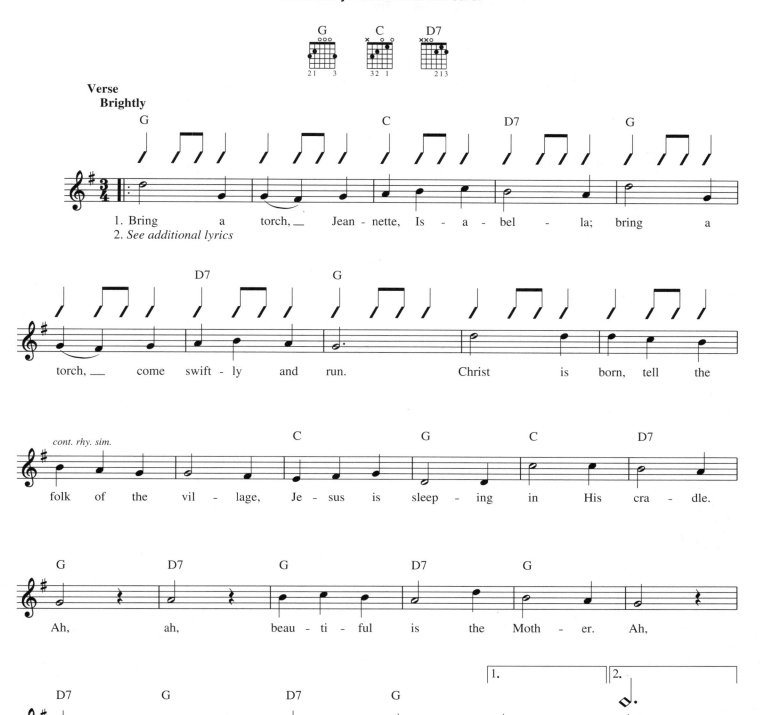

Additional Lyrics

2. Hasten now, good folk of the village,
Hasten now, the Christ Child to see.
You will find him asleep in a manger,
Quietly come and whisper softly.
Hush, hush, peacefully how He slumbers,
Hush, hush, peacefully how He sleeps.

Because It's Christmas
(For All the Children)

Music by Barry Manilow
Lyric by Bruce Sussman and Jack Feldman

Additional Lyrics

2. Tonight belongs to all the children.
   Tonight their joy rings through the air.
   And so, we send our tender blessings
   To all the children ev'rywhere
   To see the smiles and hear the laughter,
   A time to give, a time to share
   Because it's Christmas for now and forever
   For all of the children in us all.

C-H-R-I-S-T-M-A-S

Words by Jenny Lou Carson
Music by Eddy Arnold

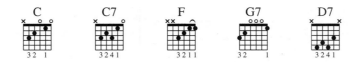

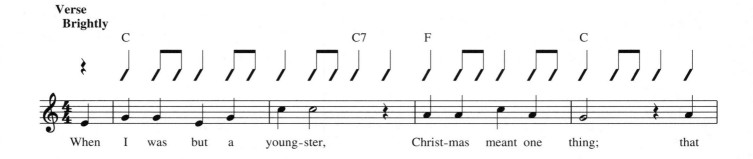

Verse
Brightly

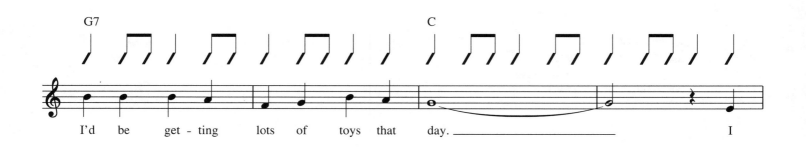

When I was but a young-ster, Christ-mas meant one thing; that

I'd be get-ting lots of toys that day. _____ I

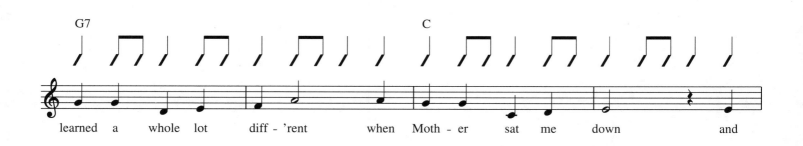

learned a whole lot diff-'rent when Moth-er sat me down and

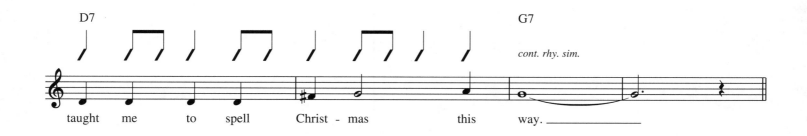

cont. rhy. sim.

taught me to spell Christ-mas this way. _____

Chorus

The Christmas Song
(Chestnuts Roasting on an Open Fire)

Music and Lyric by Mel Torme and Robert Wells

Verse
Sentimentally

1. Chest - nuts roast - ing on an o - pen fire, Jack Frost nip - ping at your nose.

Yule - tide car - ols be - ing sung by a choir and folks dressed up like Es - ki - mos. Ev - 'ry - bod - y

knows a tur - key and some mis - tle - toe help to make the sea - son bright.

Ti - ny tots with their eyes all a - glow will find it hard to sleep to -

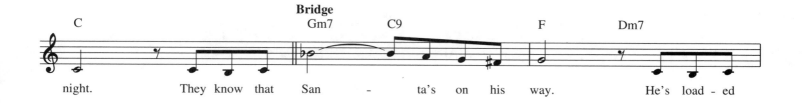

Bridge

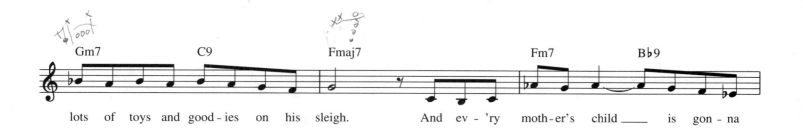

night.   They know that San - ta's on his way.   He's load - ed

lots of toys and good - ies on his sleigh.   And ev - 'ry moth - er's child ____ is gon - na

spy _____ to see if rein - deer ____ real - ly know how to fly.   2. And

Verse

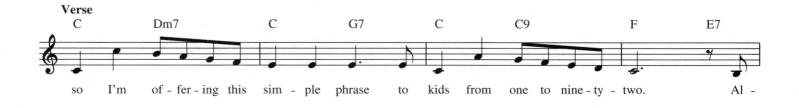

so I'm of - fer - ing this sim - ple phrase to kids from one to nine - ty - two.   Al -

though it's been said man - y times, man - y ways, "Mer - ry Christ - mas   to you."

Christmas Time Is Here

from A CHARLIE BROWN CHRISTMAS

Words by Lee Mendelson
Music by Vince Guaraldi

Coventry Carol

Words by Robert Croo
Traditional English Melody

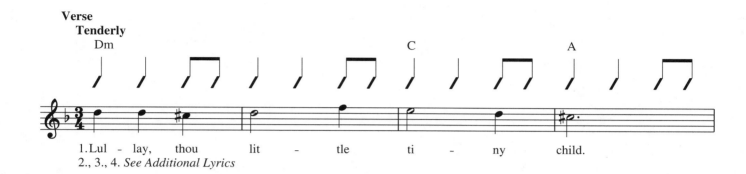

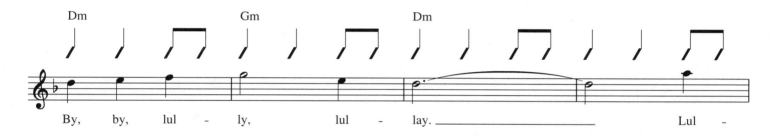

Verse
Tenderly

1.Lul - lay, thou lit - tle ti - ny child.
2., 3., 4. *See Additional Lyrics*

By, by, lul - ly, lul - lay. _____ Lul -

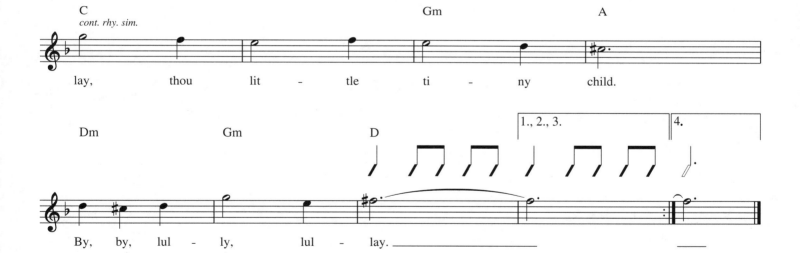

lay, thou lit - tle ti - ny child.

By, by, lul - ly, lul - lay. _____

Additional Lyrics

2. Oh, sisters too,
   How may we do,
   For to preserve this day?
   This poor youngling,
   For whom we sing
   By, by, lully lullay.

3. Herod the king,
   In his raging,
   Charged he hath this day.
   His men of might,
   In his own sight,
   All young children to slay.

4. That woe is me,
   Poor child for thee!
   And ever morn and day,
   For thy parting
   Neither say nor sing
   By, by, lully lullay!

Dance of the Sugar Plum Fairy

from THE NUTCRACKER

By Pyotr Il'yich Tchaikovsky

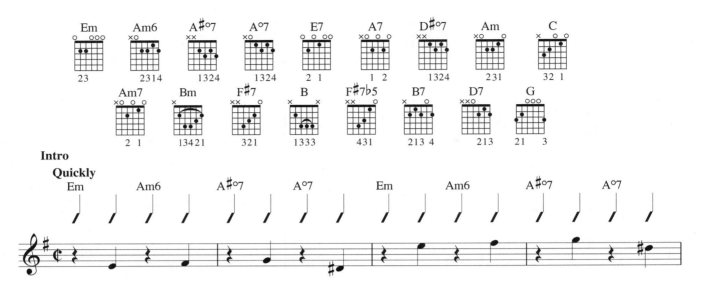

Intro
Quickly

Deck the Hall

Traditional Welsh Carol

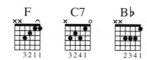

Verse
Gaily

1. Deck the hall with boughs of hol-ly; fa, la, la, la, la, la, la, la, la.
2., 3. *See additional lyrics*

'Tis the sea-son to be jol-ly; fa, la, la, la, la, la, la, la, la.

Don we now our gay ap-par-el; fa, la, la, la, la, la, la, la, la.

Troll the an-cient yule-tide car-ol; fa, la, la, la, la, la, la, la, la. la, la, la.

Additional Lyrics

2. See the blazing yule before us;
   Fa, la, la, la, la, la, la, la, la.
   Strike the harp and join the chorus;
   Fa, la, la, la, la, la, la, la, la.
   Follow me in merry measure;
   Fa, la, la, la, la, la, la, la, la.
   While I tell of Yuletide treasure.
   Fa, la, la, la, la, la, la, la, la.

3. Fast away the old year passes;
   Fa, la, la, la, la, la, la, la, la.
   Hail the new ye lads and lasses;
   Fa, la, la, la, la, la, la, la, la.
   Sing we joyous, all together;
   Fa, la, la, la, la, la, la, la, la.
   Heedless of the wind and weather;
   Fa, la, la, la, la, la, la, la, la.

Do They Know

Words and Music by Nathan Morris

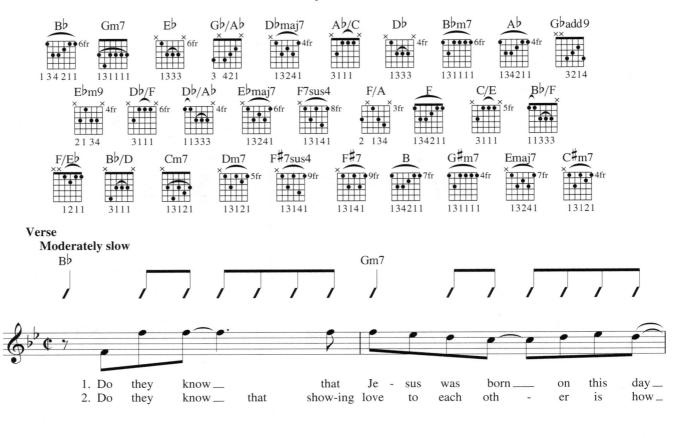

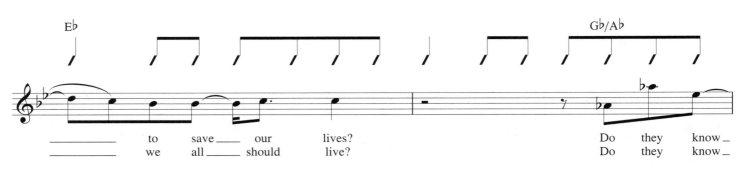

Verse
Moderately slow

1. Do they know ___ that Je - sus was born ___ on this day ___
2. Do they know ___ that show-ing love to each oth - er is how ___

___ to save ___ our lives?
___ we all ___ should live?

Do they know ___
Do they know ___

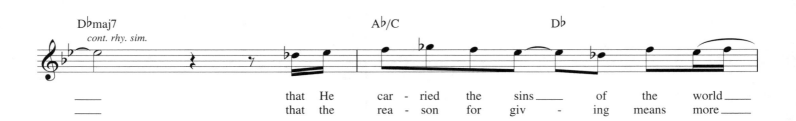

___ that He car - ried the sins ___ of the world ___
___ that the rea - son for giv - ing means more ___

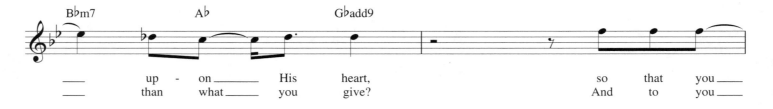

___ up - on ___ His heart, so that you ___
___ than what ___ you give? And to you ___

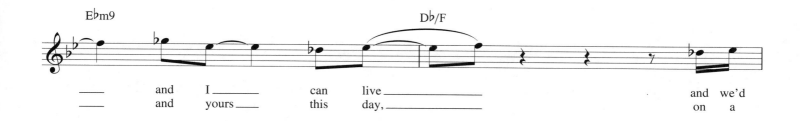

Ebm9 ... Db/F

and I can live
and yours this day, and we'd
on a

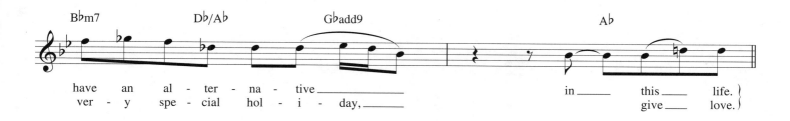

Bbm7 ... Db/Ab ... Gbadd9 ... Ab

have an al-ter-na-tive in this life.
ver-y spe-cial hol-i-day, give love.

Chorus

Bb ... Gm7

Do they know what this day means, do they know

Ebmaj7 ... F7sus4

where we've been and how it should be? Tell me, do they know?

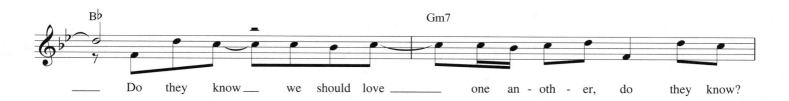

Bb ... Gm7

Do they know we should love one an-oth-er, do they know?

To Coda ⊕

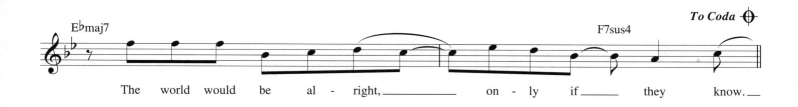

Ebmaj7 ... F7sus4

The world would be al-right, on-ly if they know.

Interlude

2nd time, D.C. al Coda

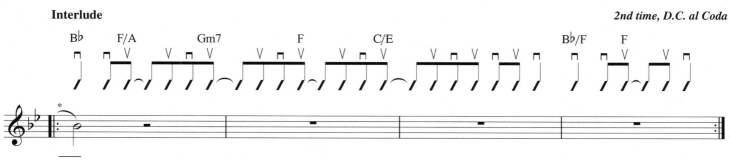

Bb F/A Gm7 F C/E Bb/F F

* Sing first time only

21

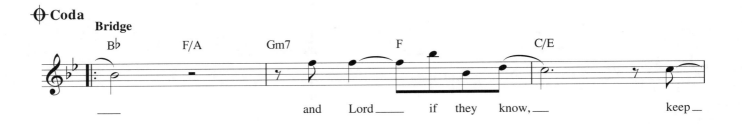

Coda

Bridge

and Lord ___ if they know, ___ keep

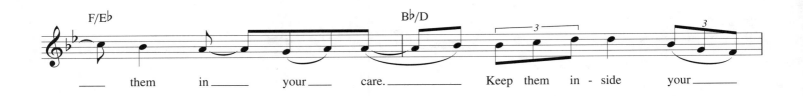

___ them in ___ your ___ care. ___ Keep them in - side your ___

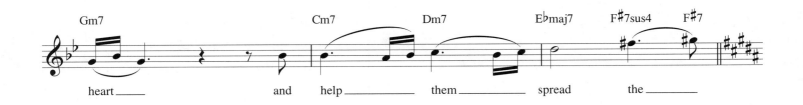

heart ___ and help ___ them ___ spread the ___

Outro-Chorus

word. Do they know ___ what ___ this day means, ___ do they know

where we've been ___ and how ___ it should be. Tell me, do ___ they ___ know?

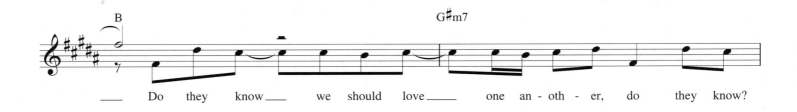

___ Do they know ___ we should love ___ one an - oth - er, do they know?

Repeat and fade

The world would be al - right, on - ly if ___ they know.

Do They Know It's Christmas?

Words and Music by M. Ure and B. Geldof

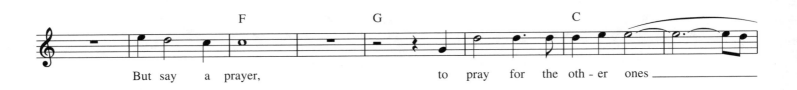

But say a prayer, to pray for the oth - er ones _____

____ at Christ - mas - time. It's hard, but ___ when you're hav - ing fun _____

____ there's ___ a ____ world out - side your win - dow, ___ and it's a

world of _____ dread and fear ____ where the on - ly wa - ter

flow - ing is _____ the bit - ter sting of tears. And the

Christ - mas bells ___ that ring ___ there _ are the clang - ing chimes of doom. _

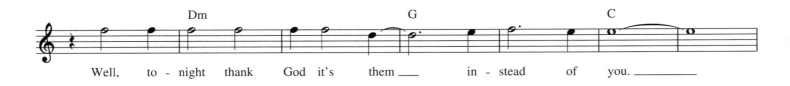

Well, to - night thank God it's them ___ in - stead of you. _____

And there won't be snow ___ in Af - ri - ca _____ this Christ -

- mas - time, ___ the great - est gift _____ they'll

Do You Hear What I Hear

Words and Music by Noel Regney and Gloria Shayne

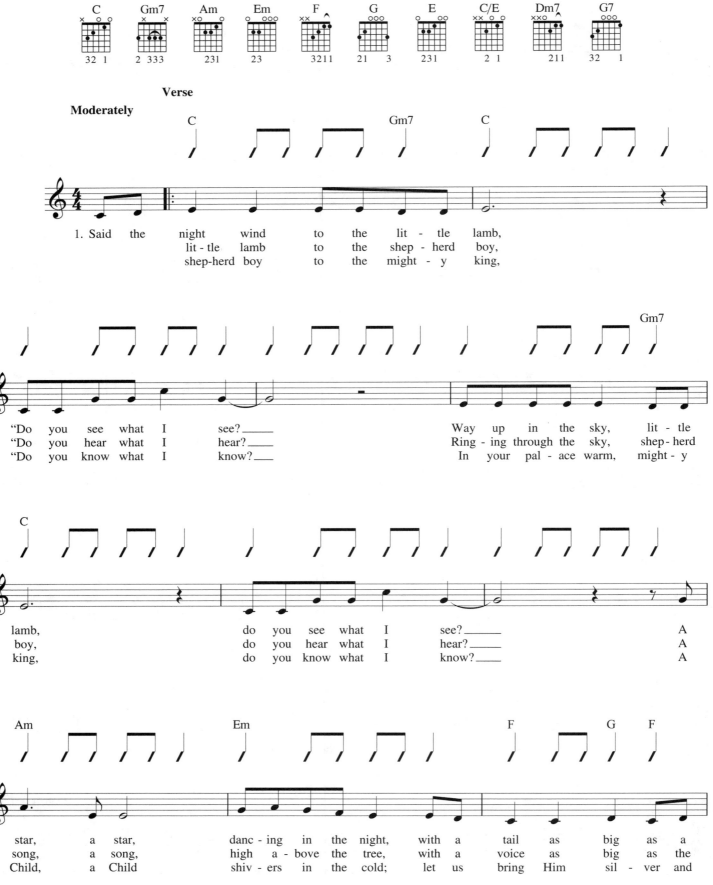

kite,
sea,
gold,

with a tail as big as a kite."
with a voice as big as the sea."
let us bring Him sil - ver and gold."

1., 2.

2. Said the
3. Said the

3.

Verse

4. Said the king to the peo - ple ev - 'ry -

where,

cont. rhy. sim.

"Lis - ten to what I say! _____

Pray for peace, peo - ple ev - 'ry - where.

lis - ten to what I say! ____

____ The Child, the Child, sleep - ing in the night, He will

bring us good - ness and light, He will bring us good - ness and

light." _____

27

Feliz Navidad

Music and Lyrics by Jose Feliciano

Go, Tell It on the Mountain

African-American Spiritual
Verses by John W. Work, Jr.

Additional Lyrics

2. The shepherds feared and trembled
   When, lo! above the earth
   Rang out the angel chorus
   That hailed our Savior's birth.

3. Down in a lowly manger
   Our humble Christ was born.
   And God sent us salvation
   That blessed Christmas morn.

The First Noël

17th Century English Carol
Music from W. Sandys' Christmas Carols

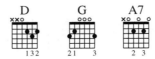

Verse
Moderately slow

1. The ___ first _____ No - ël, the ___ an - gel did

2. - 5. See additional lyrics

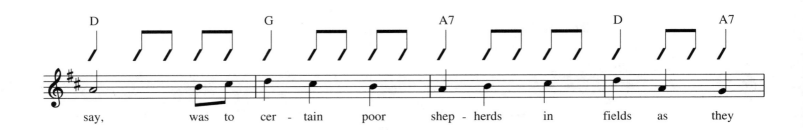

say, was to cer - tain poor shep - herds in fields as they

cont. rhy. sim.

lay. In ___ fields _____ where __ they lay ___ keep - ing their

sheep, on a cold win - ter's night ___ that was ___ so deep. No -

Chorus

ël, _____ No - ël, No - ël, No - ël,

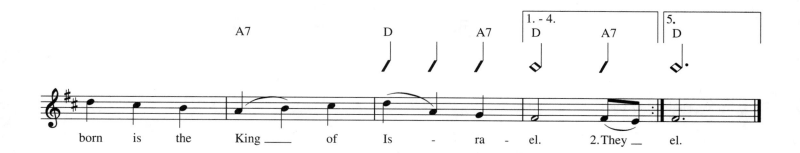

born is the King ____ of Is - ra - el. 2. They _ el.

Additional Lyrics

2. They looked up and saw a star
   Shining in the East, beyond them far.
   And to the earth it gave great light
   And so it continued both day and night.

3. And by the light of that same star,
   Three wise men came from country far;
   To seek for a King was their intent,
   And to follow the star wherever it went.

4. This star drew nigh to the northwest,
   O'er Bethlehem it took it's rest;
   And there it did both stop and stay,
   Right over the place where Jesus lay.

5. Then entered in those wise men three,
   Full reverently upon their knee;
   And offered there in His presence,
   Their gold, and myrrh, and frankincense.

Frosty the Snow Man

Words and Music by Steve Nelson and Jack Rollins

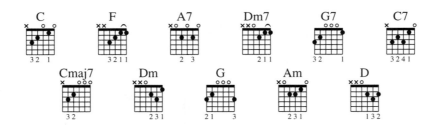

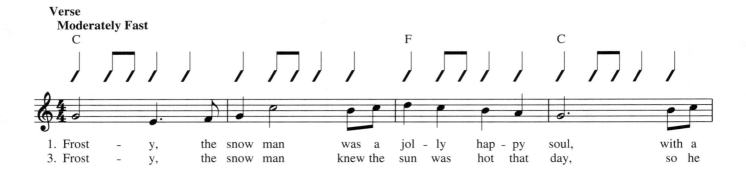

Verse
Moderately Fast

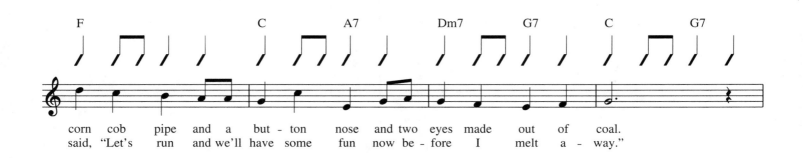

1. Frost - y, the snow man was a jol - ly hap - py soul, with a
3. Frost - y, the snow man knew the sun was hot that day, so he

corn cob pipe and a but - ton nose and two eyes made out of coal.
said, "Let's run and we'll have some fun now be - fore I melt a - way."

cont. rhy. sim.

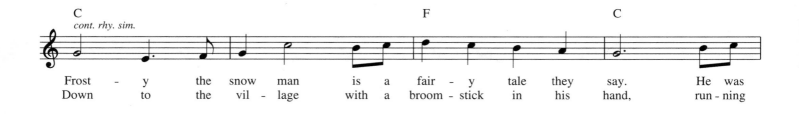

Frost - y the snow man is a fair - y tale they say. He was
Down to the vil - lage with a broom - stick in his hand, run - ning

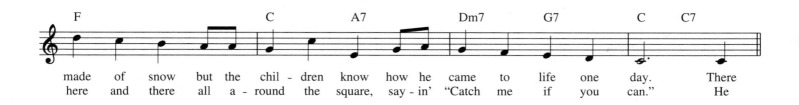

made of snow but the chil - dren know how he came to life one day. There
here and there all a - round the square, say - in' "Catch me if you can." He

Bridge

must have been some mag - ic in that old silk hat they found, for
let them down the streets of town right to the traf - fic cop, and he

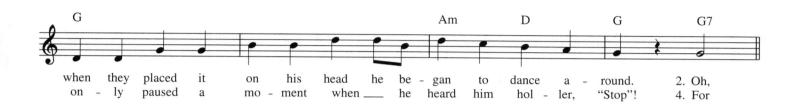

when they placed it on his head he be - gan to dance a - round. 2. Oh,
on - ly paused a mo - ment when ___ he heard him hol - ler, "Stop"! 4. For

Verse

Frost - y the snow - man was a - live as he could be, and the
Frost - y the snow - man had to hur - ry on his way, but he

chil - dren say he could laugh and play just the same as you and me.
waved good - bye say - in' "Don't you cry, I'll be back a - gain some day."

Outro

Thump - et - y thump thump, thump - et - y thump thump, look at Frost - y go.

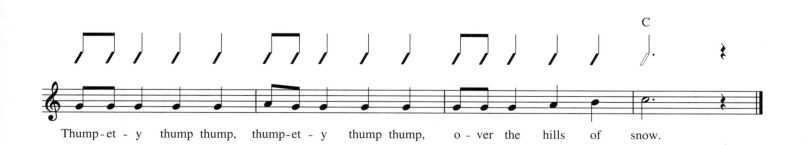

Thump - et - y thump thump, thump - et - y thump thump, o - ver the hills of snow.

God Rest Ye Merry, Gentlemen

19th Century English Carol

Verse
Moderately

1. God rest ye mer - ry, gen - tle - men, let noth - ing you dis - may. For
2. *See additional lyrics*

Je - sus Christ our Sav - ior was born up - on this day, to

save us all from Sa - tan's power when we were gone a - stray. O ____

Chorus

tid - ings of com - fort and joy, com - fort and joy. O ____

tid - ings of com - fort and joy! 2. In joy!

Additional Lyrics

2. In Bethlehem, in Jewry
This blessed babe was born
And laid within a manger
Upon this blessed morn
To which His mother Mary
Did nothing take in scorn.

Good King Wenceslas

Words by John M. Neale
Music from Piae Cantiones

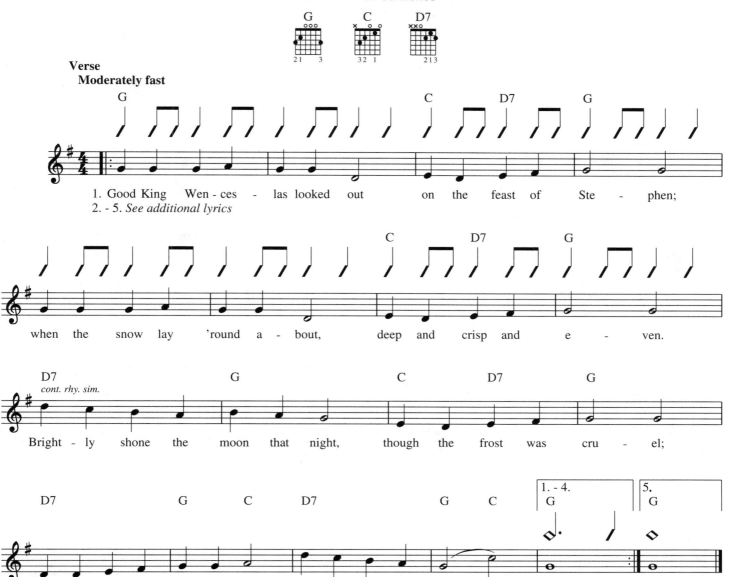

Verse
Moderately fast

1. Good King Wen - ces - las looked out on the feast of Ste - phen;
2. - 5. *See additional lyrics*

when the snow lay 'round a - bout, deep and crisp and e - ven.

Bright - ly shone the moon that night, though the frost was cru - el;

when a poor man came in sight, gath - 'ring win - ter fu - el. ing.

Additional Lyrics

2. "Hither page, and stand by me,
   If thou know'st it, telling;
   Yonder peasant, who is he?
   Where and what his dwelling?"
   "Sire, he lives a good league hence,
   Underneath the mountain;
   Right against the forest fence,
   By Saint Agnes' fountain."

3. "Bring me flesh, and bring me wine,
   Bring me pine-logs hither;
   Thou and I will see him dine,
   When we bear them thither."
   Page and monarch forth they went,
   Forth they went together;
   Through the rude winds wild lament,
   And the bitter weather.

4. "Sire, the night is darker now,
   And the wind blows stronger;
   Fails my heart, I know not how,
   I can go not longer."
   "Mark my footsteps, my good page,
   Tread thou in them boldly:
   Thou shalt find the winter's rage
   Freeze thy blood less coldly."

5. In his master's steps he trod,
   Where the snow lay dinted;
   Heat was in the very sod
   Which the saint has printed.
   Therefore, Christian men, be sure,
   Wealth or rank possessing;
   Ye who now will bless the poor,
   Shall yourselves find blessing.

Grandma Got Run Over
by a Reindeer

Words and Music by Randy Brooks

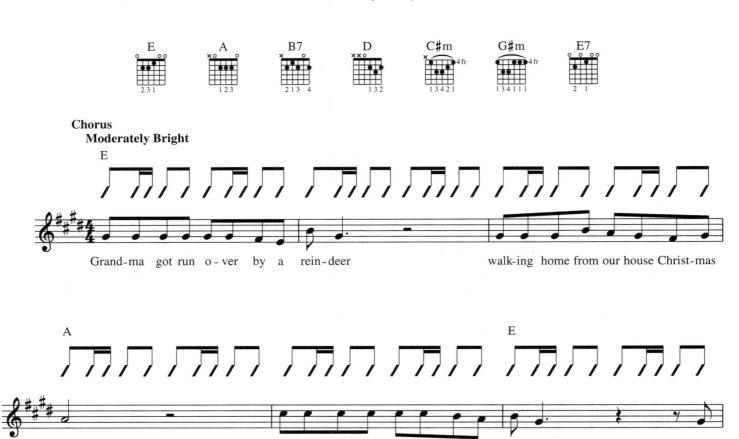

Chorus
Moderately Bright

Grand-ma got run o-ver by a rein-deer   walk-ing home from our house Christ-mas

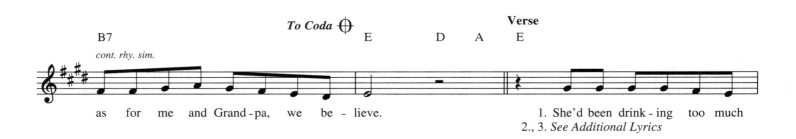

Eve.   You can   say there's no such thing as   San-ta,   but

To Coda ⊕   **Verse**

as   for   me   and   Grand-pa,   we   be - lieve.   1. She'd been drink-ing   too much
2., 3. *See Additional Lyrics*

egg - nog   and   we begged her   not   to   go.

But   she   for - got   her   med - i - ca - tion,   and   she   stag-gered out   the   door   in - to   the

Additional Lyrics

2. Now we're all so proud of Grandpa.
   He's been taking it so well.
   See him in there watching football,
   Drinking beer and playing cards with Cousin Mel.
   It's not Christmas without Grandma.
   All the family's dressed in black,
   And we just can't help but wonder:
   Should we open up her gifts or send them back?

3. Now the goose is on the table,
   And the pudding made of fig.
   And the blue and silver candles,
   That would just have matched the hair in Grandma's wig.
   I've warned all my friends and neighbors.
   Better watch out for yourselves.
   They should never give a license
   To a man who drives a sleigh and plays with elves.

Grandma's Killer Fruitcake

Words and Music by Elmo Shropshire and Rita Abrams

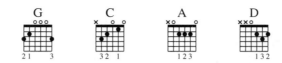

Intro
Country Polka

1. The
2., 3. *See Additional Lyrics*

Verse

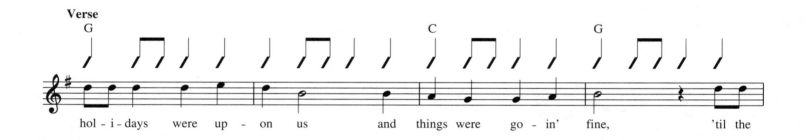

hol - i - days were up - on us and things were go - in' fine, 'til the

day I heard the door - bell and a chill ran up my spine. I

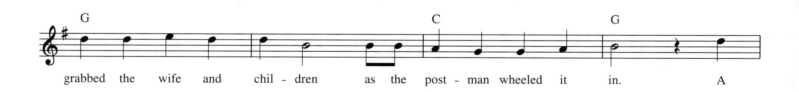

grabbed the wife and chil - dren as the post - man wheeled it in. A

year - ly Christ - mas night - mare has just come back a - gain. It was

Chorus

hard - er than the head of Un - cle Buck - y, heav - y as a Ser - mon of

Preach - er Luck - y. One's e - nough to give the whole state of Ken - tuck - y a

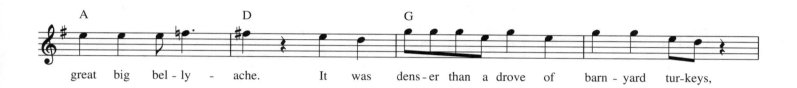

great big bel - ly - ache. It was dens - er than a drove of barn - yard tur - keys,

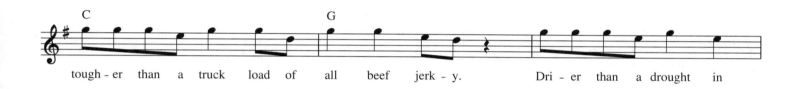

tough - er than a truck load of all beef jerk - y. Dri - er than a drought in

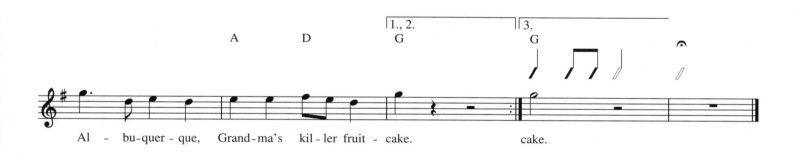

Al - bu - quer - que, Grand - ma's kil - ler fruit - cake.   cake.

Additional Lyrics

2. Now I've had to swallow some marginal fare at our family feast.
   I even downed Aunt Dolly's possom pie just to keep the family peace.
   I winced at Wilma's gizzard mousse, but said it tasted fine,
   But that lethal weapon that Grandma bakes is where I draw the line.

3. It's early Christmas morning, the phone rings us awake.
   It's Grandma, Pa, she wants to know how'd we like the cake.
   "Well, Grandma, I never. Uh, we couldn't. It was, uh, unbelievable, that's for shore.
   What's that you say? Oh, no Grandma, Puh-leez don't send us more!"

The Greatest Gift of All

Words and Music by John Jarvis

Through the win - dow I ___ can see ___ snow be - gin to fall.

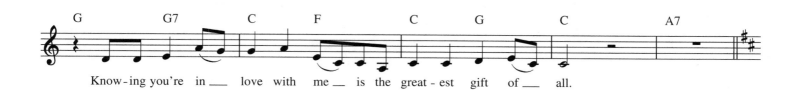

Know-ing you're in ___ love with me ___ is the great-est gift of ___ all.

Verse

3. Just be - fore I go to sleep _____ I hear a church bell ring.

Mer - ry Christ - mas ev - 'ry - one _____ is the song it ___ sings.

So I say a si - lent prayer _____ for crea - tures great and small.

Peace on earth good _ will to men is the great-est gift of ___ all. Peace on earth good _

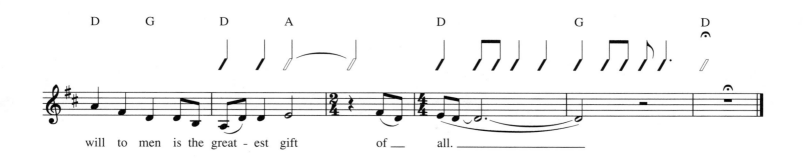

will to men is the great - est gift of ___ all. _____

Happy Holiday

from the Motion Picture Irving Berlin's HOLIDAY INN

Words and Music by Irving Berlin

Hark! The Herald Angels Sing

Words by Charles Wesley
Altered by George Whitefield
Music by Felix Mendelssohn-Bärtholdy

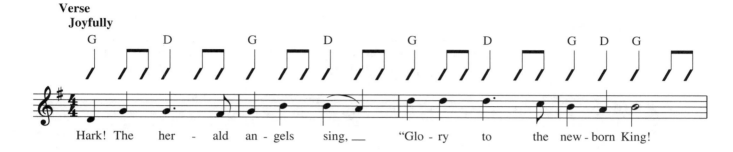

Verse
Joyfully

Hark! The her - ald an - gels sing, __ "Glo - ry to the new - born King!

Peace on earth, and mer - cy mild, __ God and sin - ners re - con - ciled."

Chorus

cont. rhy. sim.

Joy - ful all ye na - tions rise. __ Join the tri - umph of the skies. __

With th'an - gel - ic host pro - claim, "Christ is __ born in Beth - le - hem."

Hark! The her - ald an - gels sing, "Glo - ry __ to the new - born King!"

Happy Xmas (War Is Over)

Words and Music by John Lennon and Yoko Ono

A Holly Jolly Christmas

Music and Lyrics by Johnny Marks

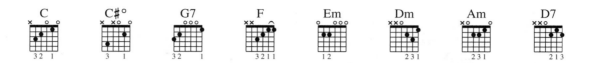

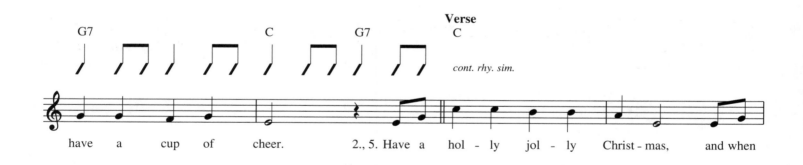

Bridge

ev - 'ry - one you meet. Oh, ho, the mis - tle - toe

hung where you can see. Some - bod - y waits for you,

Verse

kiss her once for me. 3., 6. Have a hol - ly jol - ly Christ - mas, and in

case you did - n't hear: Oh, by gol - ly, have a

1.

hol - ly jol - ly Christ - mas this year. 4. Have a

2.

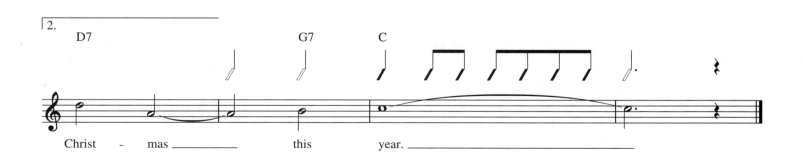

Christ - mas _____ this year. _____

(There's No Place Like)
Home for the Holidays

Words by Al Stillman
Music by Robert Allen

home-made pump-kin pie. From Penn-syl-van-ia folks are trav-'lin' down to
wel-come with your heart. From Cal-i-for-nia to New Eng-land down to

Dix-ie's sun-ny shore; } from At-lan-tic to Pa-ci-fic, gee, the
Dix-ie's sun-ny shore; }

traf-fic is ter-ri-fic. Oh, there's no place like home for the

hol-i-days, _____ 'cause no mat-ter how far a-way you roam, _____ if you

want to be hap-py in a mil-lion ways, _____ for the

hol-i-days you can't beat home, sweet home. _____ Oh, there's

can't beat home, sweet home. _____

Hymne

By Vangelis

I Heard the Bells on Christmas Day

Words by Henry Wadsworth Longfellow
Music by John Baptiste Calkin

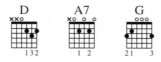

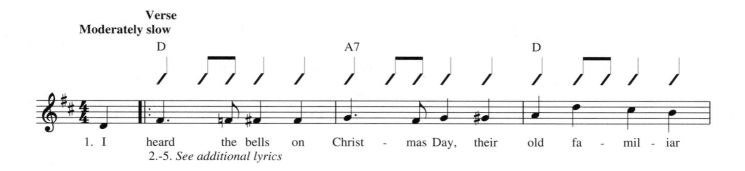

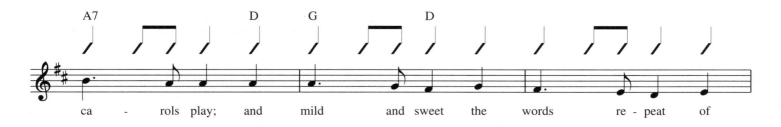

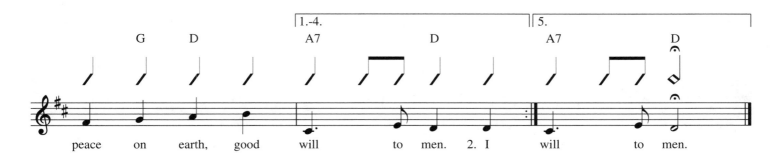

Additional Lyrics

2. I thought as now this day had come,
   The belfries of all Christendom
   Had rung so long the unbroken song
   Of peace on earth, good will to men.

3. And in despair I bow'd my head:
   "There is no peace on earth," I said,
   "For hate is strong, and mocks the song
   Of peace on earth, good will to men."

4. Then pealed the bells more loud and deep:
   "God is not dead, nor doth He sleep;
   The wrong shall fail, the right prevail,
   With peace on earth, good will to men."

5. Till ringing, singing on it's way,
   The world revolved from night to day,
   Avoice, a chime, a chant sublime,
   Of peace on earth, good will to men!"

I Saw Mommy Kissing Santa Claus

Words and Music by Tommie Connor

I Saw Three Ships

Traditional English Carol

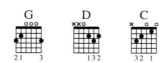

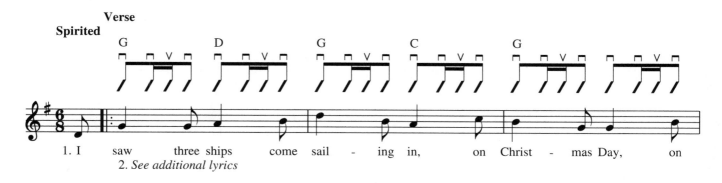

Verse
Spirited

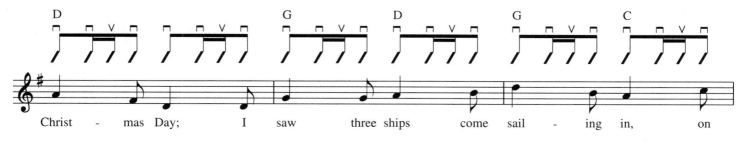

1. I saw three ships come sail - ing in, on Christ - mas Day, on
2. See additional lyrics

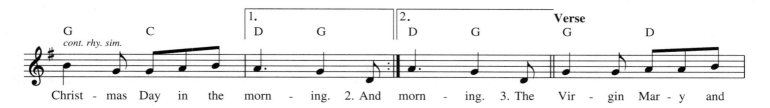

Christ - mas Day; I saw three ships come sail - ing in, on

Christ - mas Day in the morn - ing. 2. And morn - ing. 3. The Vir - gin Mar - y and

Christ were there, on Christ - mas Day, on Christ - mas Day; The

Vir - gin Mar - y and Christ were there, on Christ - mas Day in the morn - ing.

Additional Lyrics

2. And what was in those ships, all three,
On Christmas Day, on Christmas Day;
And what was in those ships, all three,
On Christmas Day in the morning.

I'll Be Home for Christmas

Words and Music by Kim Gannon and Walter Kent

It Came Upon the Midnight Clear

Words by Edmund H. Sears
Traditional English Melody
Adapted by Arthur Sullivan

Verse
Quietly

It came up-on ____ the mid - night clear, that glo - rious song ____ of old, ____ from an - gels bend - ing near the earth to touch their harps ____ of

Chorus

gold. _____ "Peace on the earth, ____ good will to men, from

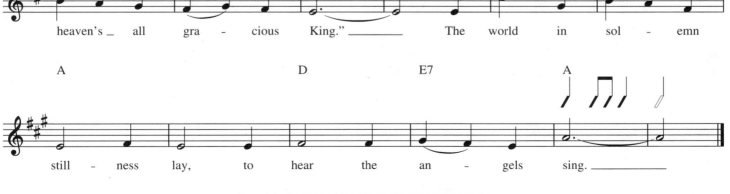

heaven's _ all gra - cious King." _____ The world in sol - emn still - ness lay, to hear the an - gels sing. _____

I'm Spending Christmas With You

Words and Music by Tom Occhipinti

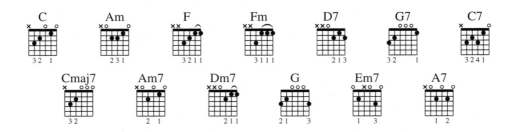

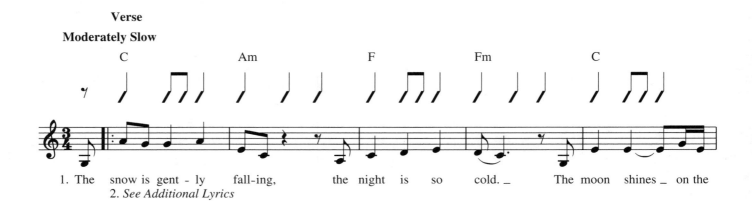

Verse
Moderately Slow

1. The snow is gent - ly fall-ing, the night is so cold. _ The moon shines _ on the
2. *See Additional Lyrics*

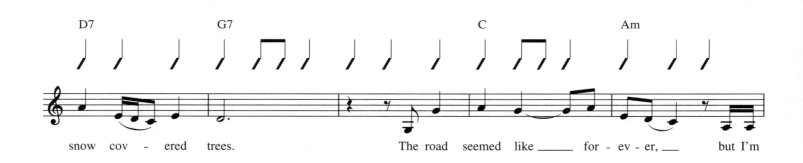

snow cov - ered trees. The road seemed like _____ for - ev - er, ___ but I'm

fi - nal - ly home. _ We're a - lone on this Christ - mas Eve.

%S **Chorus**

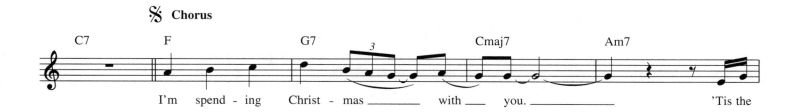

I'm spend - ing Christ - mas _____ with ___ you. _____ 'Tis the

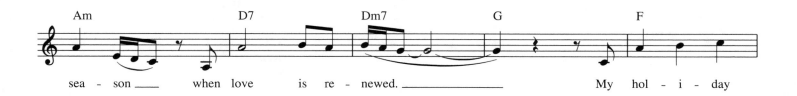

sea - son ___ when love is re - newed. _____ My hol - i - day

To Coda ⊕

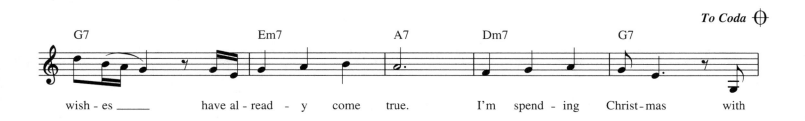

wish - es _____ have al - read - y come true. I'm spend - ing Christ - mas with

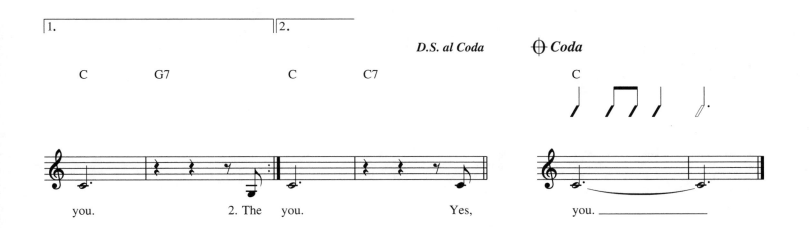

D.S. al Coda   ⊕ *Coda*

you.   2. The you.   Yes,   you. _____

Additional Lyrics

2. The fireplace is burning and your hands feel so warm.
   We're hanging popcorn on the tree.
   I take you in my arms, your lips touch mine.
   It feels like our first Christmas Eve.

I've Got My Love to Keep Me Warm

from the 20th Century Fox Motion Picture ON THE AVENUE

Words and Music by Irving Berlin

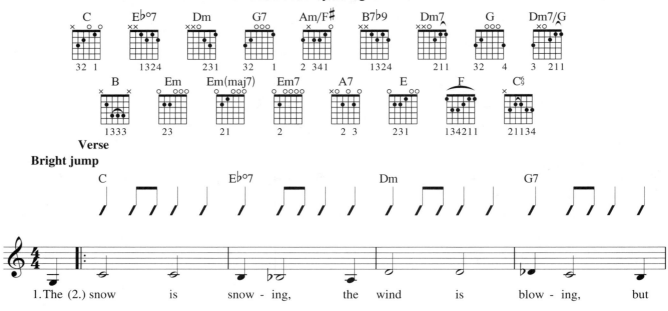

Verse

Bright jump

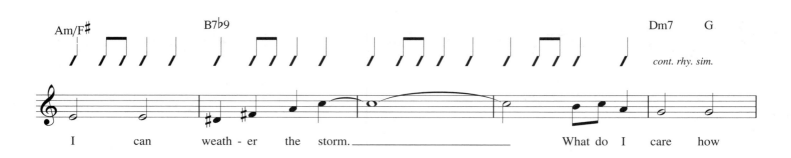

1.The (2.) snow is snow - ing, the wind is blow - ing, but

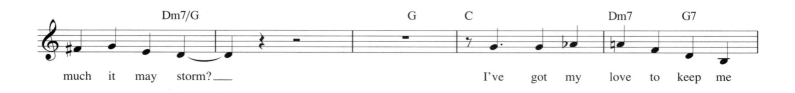

I can weath - er the storm. _____ What do I care how

much it may storm? ___ I've got my love to keep me

warm. _____ I can't re - mem - ber a worse De - cem - ber; just

watch those i - ci - cles form. _____ What do I care if i - ci - cles form? ___

I've got my love to keep me warm.

Bridge

Off with my o - ver - coat, ___ off with my glove.

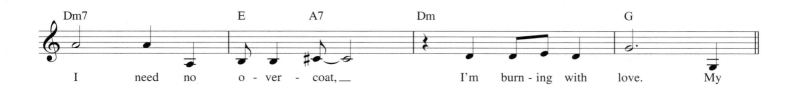

I need no o - ver - coat, ___ I'm burn - ing with love. My

Outro-Verse

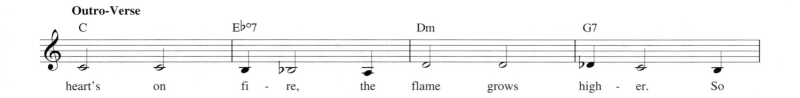

heart's on fi - re, the flame grows high - er. So

I will weath - er the storm. _____ What do I care how

much it may storm? _____ I've got my

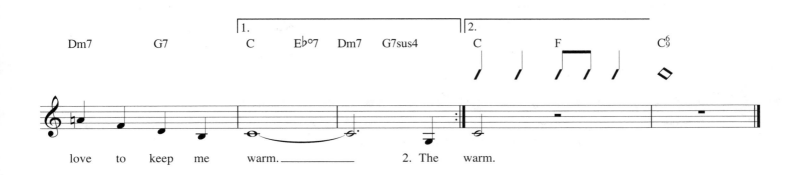

love to keep me warm. _____ 2. The warm.

It Must Have Been the Mistletoe
(Our First Christmas)

By Justin Wilde and Doug Konecky

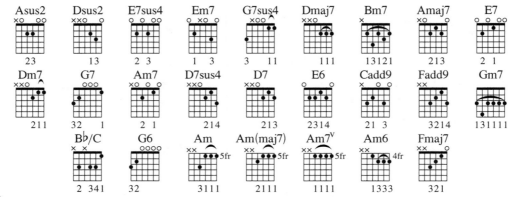

Verse

Moderately

1. It must have been ___ the mis - tle - toe, ___ the la - zy fire, ___ the fall - ing snow, ___ the

ma - gic in ___ the frost - y air, ___ that feel - ing ev - 'ry - where. It

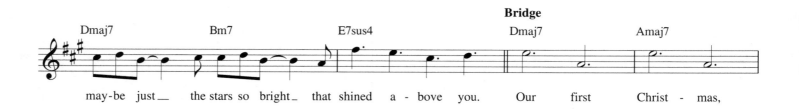

must have been ___ the pret - ty lights ___ that glis - tened ___ in the si - lent night, ___ or

Bridge

may - be just ___ the stars so bright ___ that shined a - bove you. Our first Christ - mas,

Bm7   E7   Amaj7   Dm7   G7   Em7   Am7

more than __ we'd been dream - ing of. _____ Old Saint Nich - 'las

D7sus4   D7   E7sus4   E7

had his fin - gers crossed, that we would fall in love. __ 2. It

Verse

Asus2

could have been __ the hol - i - day, __ the mid - night ride __ up - on a sleigh, __ the

Dsus2   E7sus4

coun - try - side __ all dressed in white, __ that cra - zy snow - ball fight. It

Asus2   Em7   G7sus4

could have been __ the stee - ple bell __ that wrapped us up with - in its spell. __ It

Dmaj7   Bm7   E7sus4   E6

on - ly took one kiss to know, __ it must have been the

Bridge

Asus2   Dmaj7   Amaj7

mis - tle - toe. Our first Christ - mas,

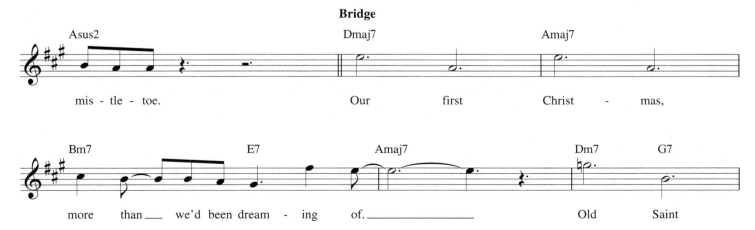

Bm7   E7   Amaj7   Dm7   G7

more than __ we'd been dream - ing of. _____ Old Saint

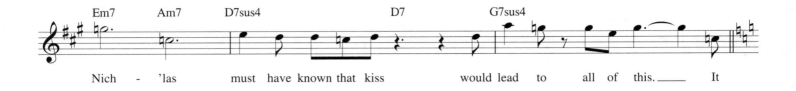

Nich - 'las   must have known that kiss   would lead   to   all of this. ___ It

Outro-Verse

must have been ___   the mis - tle - toe, ___   the la - zy fire, ___   the fall - ing snow, _ the

mag - ic in ___   the frost - y air, ___   that made   me   love   you.   On

Christ - mas Eve ___   a wish come true, ___   that night I ___   fell in love with you. ___   It

on - ly took ___   one kiss to know, ___   it must   have   been   the

mis - tle - toe!   It must   have   been   the mis - tle - toe!   It

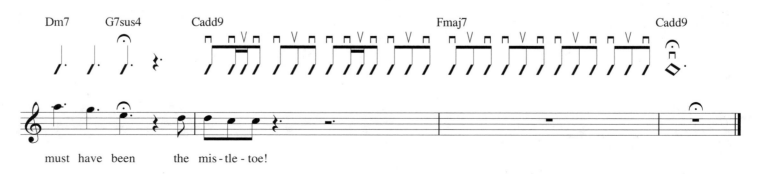

must have been   the mis - tle - toe!

It's Beginning to Look Like Christmas

By Meredith Willson

It's Christmas in New York

Words and Music by Billy Butt

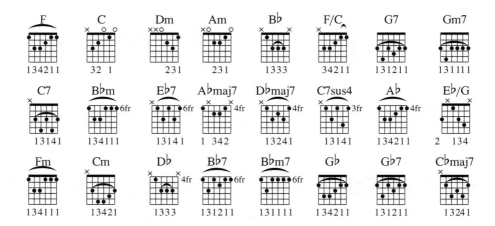

Verse

Moderately

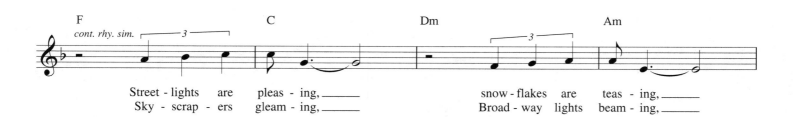

1. Church-bells are ring-ing, _____ choirs are sing-ing, _____
2. Rest-'rant signs sway-ing, _____ blue skies are gray-ing, _____

joy they are bring-ing, _____ it's Christ-mas in New York.
ev-'ry-one's say-ing, _____ it's Christ-mas in New York.

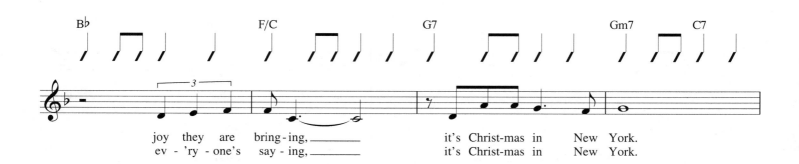

Street-lights are pleas-ing, _____ snow-flakes are teas-ing, _____
Sky-scrap-ers gleam-ing, _____ Broad-way lights beam-ing, _____

Cen-tral Park's freez-ing, _____ it's Christ-mas in New York. The
chil-dren are dream-ing, _____ it's Christ-mas in New York. The

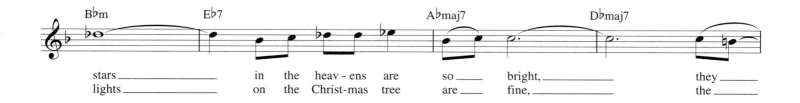

stars _____ in the heav - ens are so _____ bright, _____ they _____
lights _____ on the Christ-mas tree are _____ fine, _____ the _____

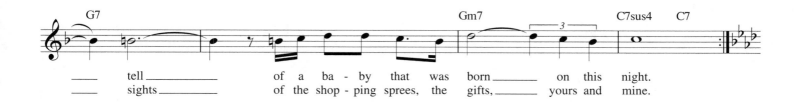

_____ tell _____ of a ba - by that was born _____ on this night.
_____ sights _____ of the shop - ping sprees, the gifts, _____ yours and mine.

Verse

3. Stock - ings are fill - ing, _____ cham - pagne is chill - ing, _____

it's all so thrill - ing _____ it's Christ-mas in New York.

Log fires are burn - ing, _____ San - ta's re - turn - ing _____

fill - ing each yearn - ing, _____ it's Christ-mas in New_ York.

Interlude

Outro-Verse

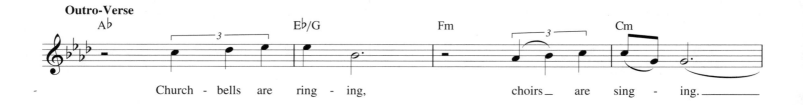

Church - bells are ring - ing, choirs__ are sing - ing._____

____ joy they are bring - ing,_____ it's Christ - mas in New

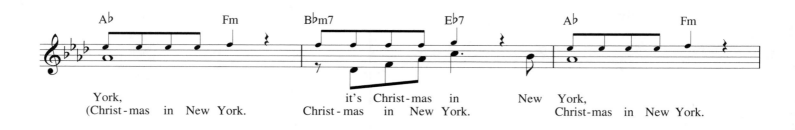

York, it's Christ - mas in New York,
(Christ - mas in New York. Christ - mas in New York. Christ - mas in New York.

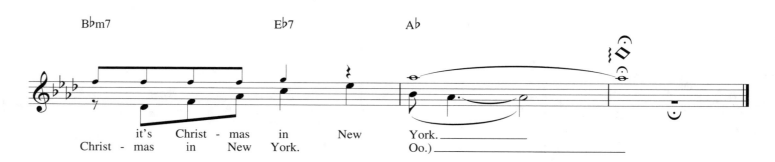

it's Christ - mas in New York._____
Christ - mas in New York. Oo.)_____

Jesus Is Born

Words and Music by Steve Green, Phil Naish and Colleen Green

Intro
Joyfully

1., 2., 3. The bells are ring - ing, peo - ple are sing - ing,

an - gels say with joy, "Je - sus is born!" There in a man - ger,

D.S. al Coda
(take 2nd ending)

Coda   **Verse**

Bridge

Christ has fi – nal – ly come. Glo – ry to __ the King, let the peo – ple sing

Hal – le – lu – jah, ____ Hal – le – lu – jah. ____

Verse

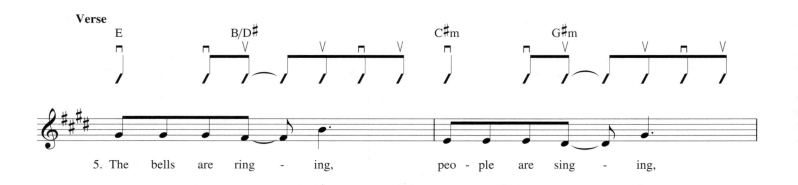

5. The bells are ring – ing, peo – ple are sing – ing,

an – gels say with joy, "Je – sus is born!" There in a man – ger,

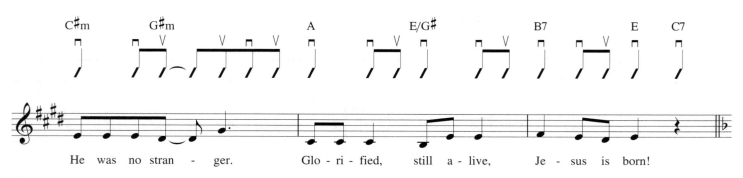

He was no stran – ger. Glo – ri – fied, still a – live, Je – sus is born!

Jingle-Bell Rock

Words and Music by Joe Beal and Jim Boothe

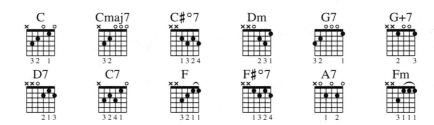

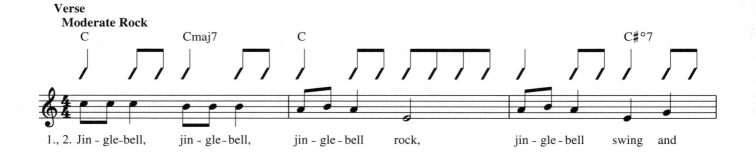

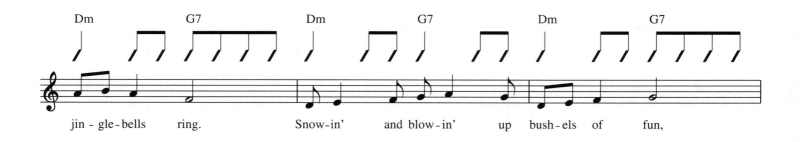

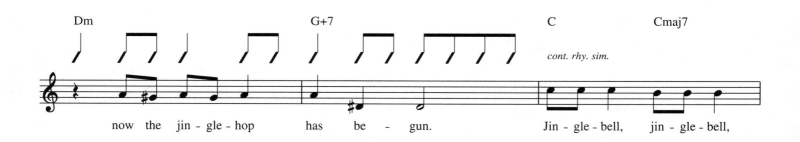

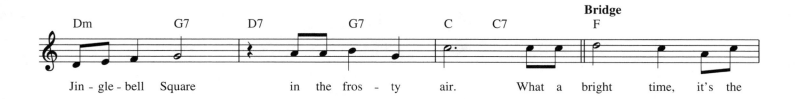

Jin - gle - bell Square in the fros - ty air. What a bright time, it's the

right time to rock the night a - way. Jin - gle - bell time is a

swell time to go gli - din' in a one horse sleigh.

Outro

Gid - dy - ap, jin - gle horse pick up your feet, jin - gle a - round the clock.

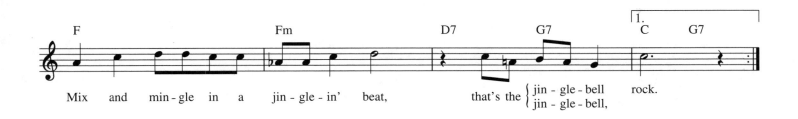

Mix and min - gle in a jin - gle - in' beat, that's the { jin - gle - bell rock.
{ jin - gle - bell,

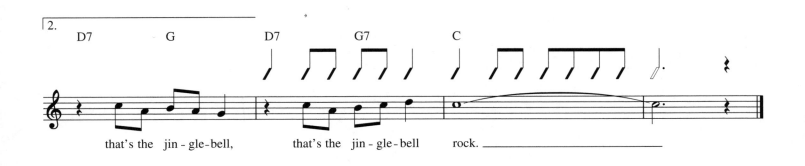

that's the jin - gle - bell, that's the jin - gle - bell rock. _____

Jingle Bells

Words and Music by J. Pierpont

Verse
Brightly

1. Dash - ing through the snow, in a one horse o - pen sleigh.
2., 3. *See Additional Lyrics*

O'er the fields we go, laugh - ing all the way.

cont. rhy. sim.

Bells on bob - tail ring, mak - ing spir - its bright. What

fun it is to ride and sing a sleigh - ing song to - night! Oh!

Chorus

Jin - gle bells, jin - gle bells, jin - gle all the way.

Oh, what fun it is to ride in a one horse o - pen sleigh! _____

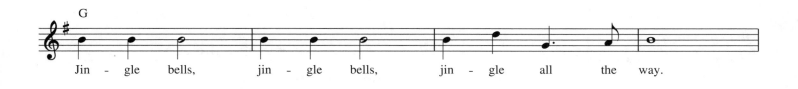

Jin - gle bells, jin - gle bells, jin - gle all the way.

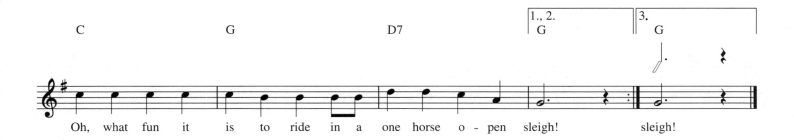

Oh, what fun it is to ride in a one horse o - pen sleigh! sleigh!

Additional lyrics

2. A day or two ago, I thought I'd take a ride,
   And soon Miss Fannie Bright was sitting by my side.
   The horse was lean and lank,
   Misfortune seemed his lot.
   He got into a drifted bank and we, we got upshot! Oh!

3. Now the ground is white, go it while you're young.
   Take the girls tonight and sing this sleighing song.
   Just get a bobtail bay,
   Two-forty for his speed.
   Then hitch him to an open sleigh and
   Crack, you'll take the lead! Oh!

Jolly Old St. Nicholas

Traditional 19th Century American Carol

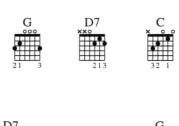

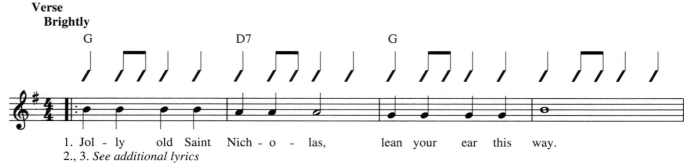

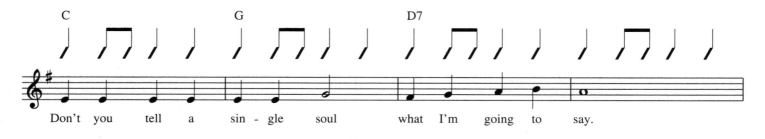

Additional Lyrics

2. When the clock is striking twelve, when I'm fast asleep.
   Down the chimney broad and black, with your pack you'll creep.
   All the stockings you will find hanging in a row.
   Mine will be the shortest one, you'll be sure to know.

3. Johnny wants a pair of skates; Susy wants a sled.
   Nellie wants a picture book, yellow, blue and red.
   Now I think I'll leave to you what to give the rest.
   Choose for me, dear Santa Claus.
   You will know the best.

Joy to the World

Words by Isaac Watts
Music by George Frideric Handel
Arranged by Lowell Mason

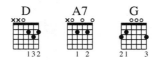

Additional Lyrics

2. He rules the world with truth and grace
   And makes the nations prove
   The glories of His righteousness
   And wonders of His love,
   And wonders of His love.
   And wonders, wonders of His love.

Last Christmas

Words and Music by George Michael

Additional Lyrics

2. A crowded room, friends with tired eyes.
   I'm hiding from you and your soul of ice.
   My God, I thought you were someone to rely on.
   Me, I guess I was a shoulder to cry on.
   A face on a lover with a fire in his heart,
   A man undercover but you tore me apart.
   Ooh, now I've found a real love.
   You'll never fool me again.

Let It Snow! Let It Snow! Let It Snow!

Words by Sammy Cahn
Music by Jule Styne

A Marshmallow World

Words by Carl Sigman
Music by Peter De Rose

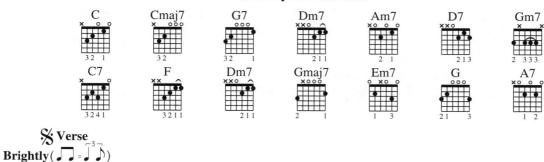

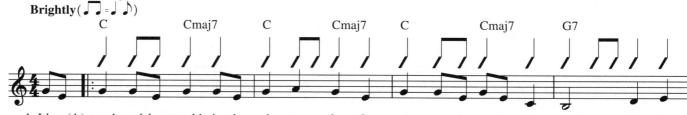

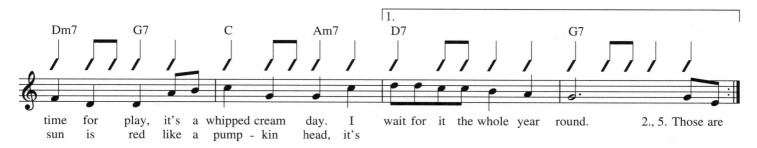

1. It's a (4.) marsh-mal-low world in the win-ter when the snow comes to cov-er the ground. It's the
marsh-mal-low clouds be-ing friend-ly in the arms of ev-er-green trees. And the

time for play, it's a whipped cream day. I wait for it the whole year round. 2., 5. Those are
sun is red like a pump-kin head, it's

shin-ing so your nose won't freeze. The world is your snow ball; see how it grows. That's how it goes, when-

ev-er it snows. The world is your snow ball; just for a song, get out and roll it a-

long. 3. It's a yum-yum-my world made for sweet hearts. Take a walk with your fa-vor-ite girl. It's a

su-gar date. What if spring is late? In win-ter, it's a marsh-mal-low world. 4. It's a

freeze.

Little Saint Nick

Words and Music by Brian Wilson and Mike Love

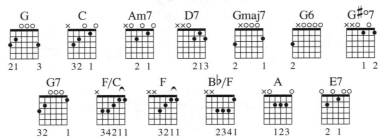

Tune down ½ step:
(low to high) E♭ - A♭ - D♭ - G♭ - B♭ - E♭

Intro
Moderately fast

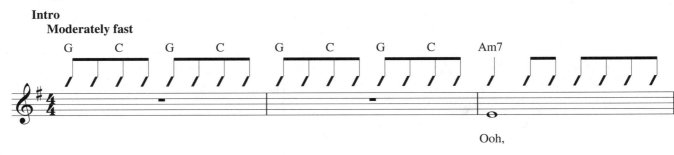

Ooh,

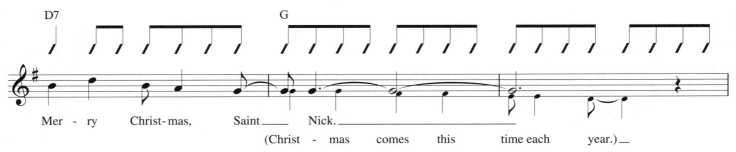

Mer-ry Christ-mas, Saint ___ Nick. _____
(Christ-mas comes this time each year.) ___

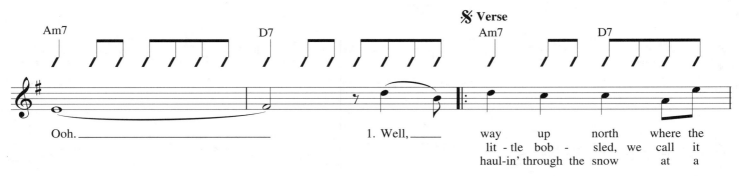

Ooh. _____ 1. Well, ___ way up north where the
lit-tle bob-sled, we call it
haul-in' through the snow at a

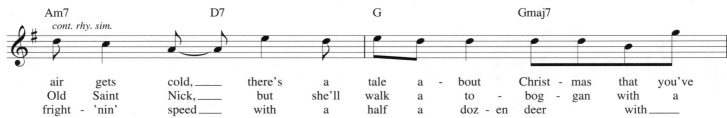

air gets cold, ___ there's a tale a-bout Christ-mas that you've
Old Saint Nick, ___ but she'll walk a to-bog-gan with a
fright-'nin' speed ___ with a half a doz-en deer with ___

all been told. ___ And a real fa-mous cat all dressed
four-speed stick. ___ She's can-dy ap-ple red with a
Ru-dy to lead. He's got-ta wear his gog-gles 'cause the

Merry Christmas, Darling

Words and Music by Richard Carpenter and Frank Pooler

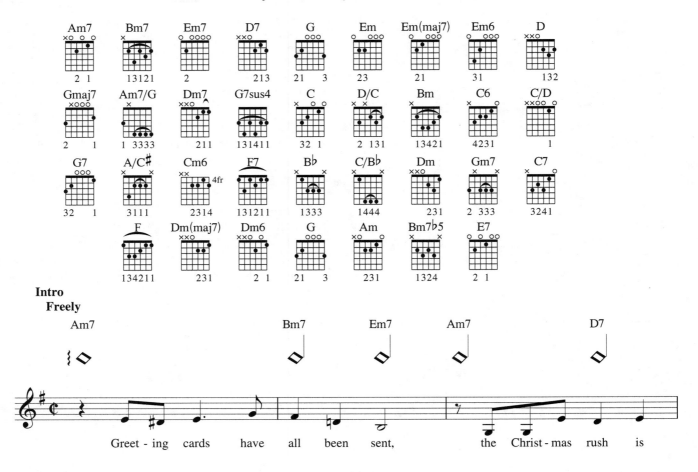

Intro
Freely

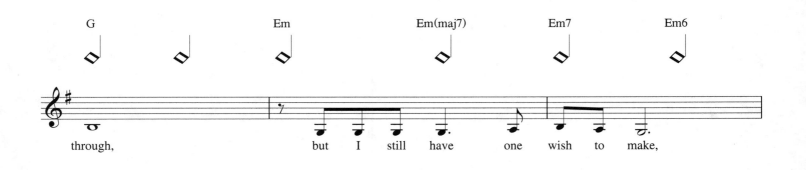

Greet-ing cards have all been sent, the Christ-mas rush is through, but I still have one wish to make,

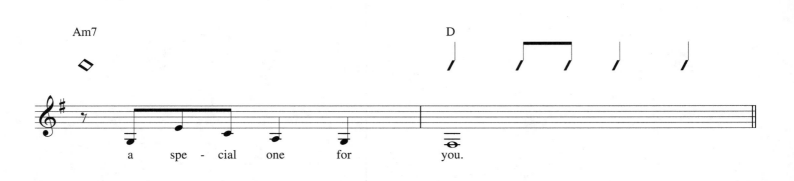

a spe-cial one for you.

Verse

Moderately slow

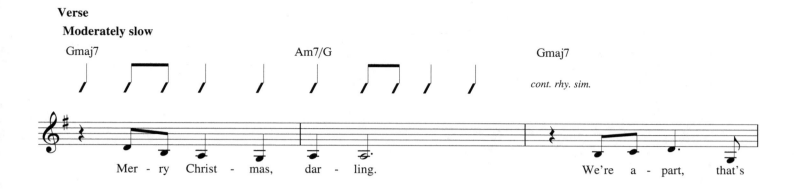

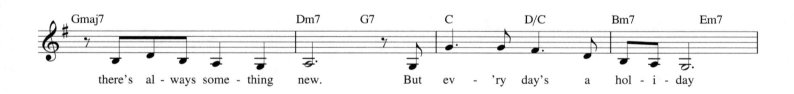

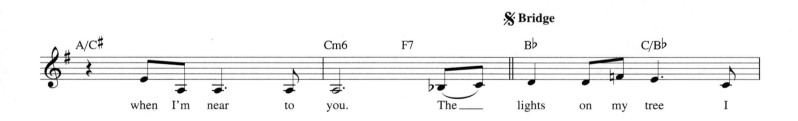

Bridge

85

logs on the fire   fill me with de - sire   to see you and to_____

Outro-Verse

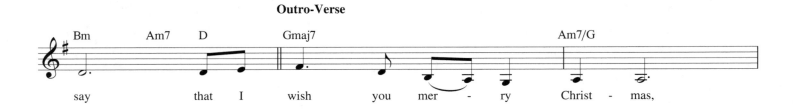

say   that I wish you mer - ry Christ - mas,

hap - py New Year too.   I've just one wish on this

To Coda ✛   *D.S. al Coda*

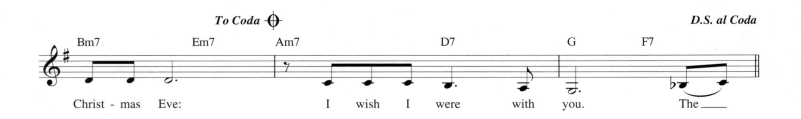

Christ - mas Eve: I wish I were with you.   The_____

✛ **Coda**

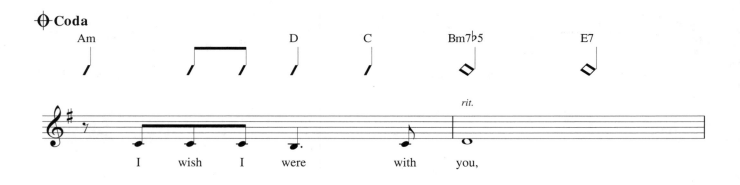

I wish I were with you,

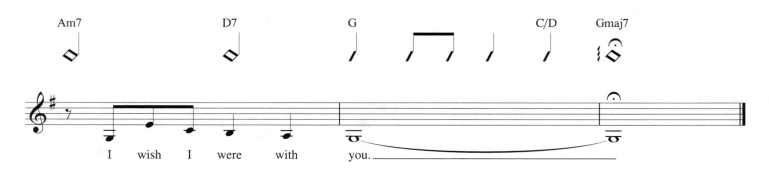

I wish I were with you._____

O Christmas Tree

Traditional German Carol

Additional Lyrics

2. O, Christmas tree! O, Christmas tree,
Much pleasure doth thou bring me!
O, Christmas tree! O, Christmas tree,
Much pleasure does thou bring me!
For every year the Christmas tree
Brings to us all both joy and glee.
O, Christmas tree, O, Christmas tree,
Much pleasure doth thou bring me!

3. O, Christmas tree! O, Christmas tree,
Thy candles shine out brightly!
O, Christmas tree, O, Christmas tree,
Thy candles shine out brightly!
Each bough doth hold its tiny light
That makes each toy to sparkle bright.
O, Christmas tree, O, Christmas tree,
Thy candles shine out brightly.

The Most Wonderful Time of the Year

Words and Music by Eddie Pola and George Wyle

Bridge

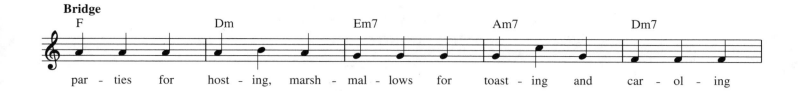

par - ties for host - ing, marsh - mal - lows for toast - ing and car - ol - ing

out in the snow. There'll be scar - y ghost stor - ies and

D.S. al Coda

tales of the glo - ries of Christ - mas - es long, long a - go. _____ 3. It's the

Coda
Outro

most won - der - ful time, it's the most won - der - ful

time. It's the most won - der - ful time _____

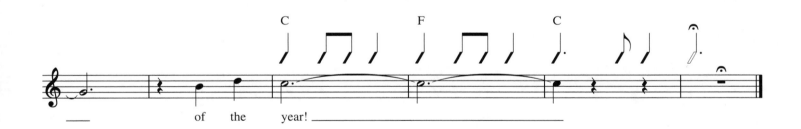

____ of the year! _____

Additional Lyrics

2. It's the hap-happiest season of all,
   With those holiday greetings
   And gay happy meetings
   When friends come to call.
   It's the hap-happiest season of all.

3. It's the most wonderful time of the year.
   There'll be much mistletoeing
   And hearts will be glowing
   When loved ones are near.
   It's the most wonderful time of the year.

My Favorite Things

from THE SOUND OF MUSIC

Lyrics by Oscar Hammerstein II
Music by Richard Rodgers

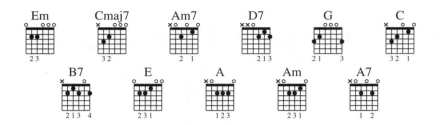

Verse
Lively, With Spirit

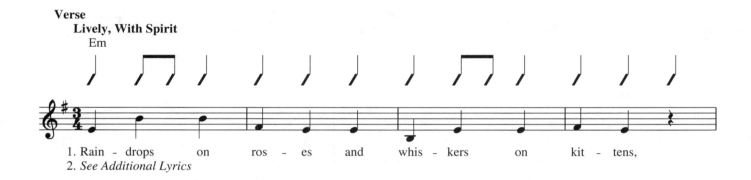

1. Rain - drops on ros - es and whis - kers on kit - tens,
2. *See Additional Lyrics*

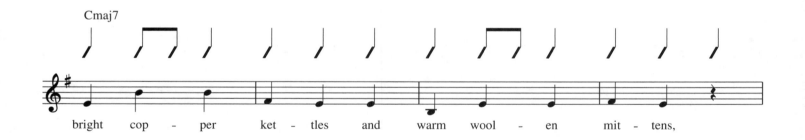

bright cop - per ket - tles and warm wool - en mit - tens,

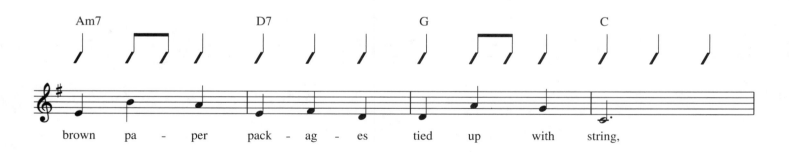

brown pa - per pack - ag - es tied up with string,

these are a few of my fa - vor - ite things.

Additional Lyrics

2. Cream colored ponies and crisp apple strudles,
   Doorbells and sleigh bells and schnitzel with noodles,
   Wild geese that fly with the moon on their wings,
   These are a few of my favorite things.

The Night Before Christmas Song

Music by Johnny Marks
Lyrics adapted by Johnny Marks from Clement Moore's Poem

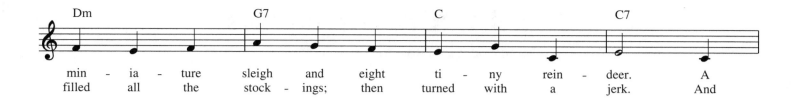

min - ia - ture sleigh and eight ti - ny rein - deer. A
filled all the stock - ings; then turned with a jerk. And

lit - tle old dri - ver so live - ly and quick, I
lay - ing his fin - ger a - side of his nose, then

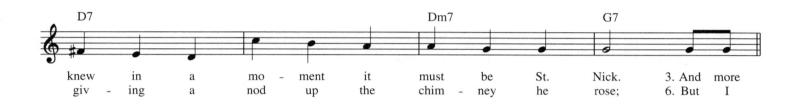

knew in a mo - ment it must be St. Nick. 3. And more
giv - ing a nod up the chim - ney he rose; 6. But I

Verse

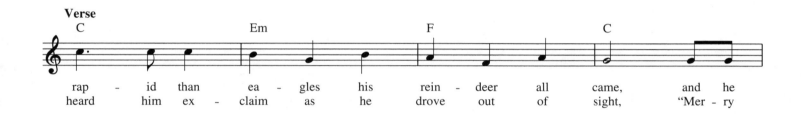

rap - id than ea - gles his rein - deer all came, and he
heard him ex - claim as he drove out of sight, "Mer - ry

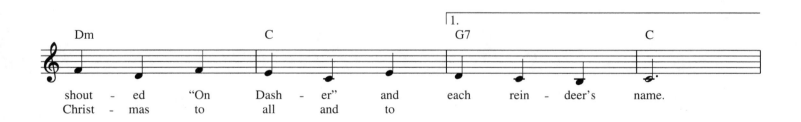

shout - ed "On Dash - er" and each rein - deer's name.
Christ - mas to all and to

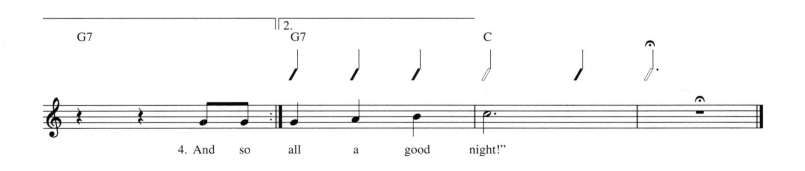

4. And so all a good night!"

Nuttin' for Christmas

Words and Music by Roy Bennett and Sid Tepper

Verse

Brightly

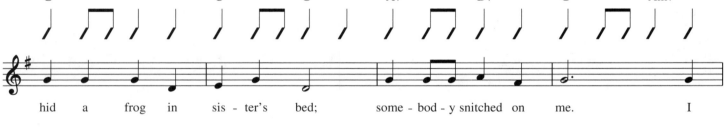

1. I broke my bat on John-ny's head; some-bod-y snitched on me. I
2., 3. *See Additional Lyrics*

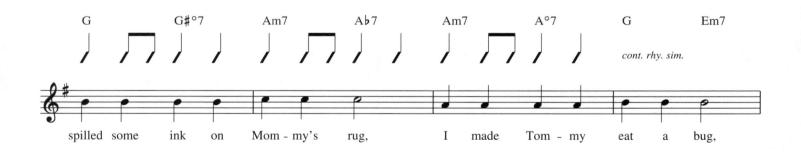

hid a frog in sis-ter's bed; some-bod-y snitched on me. I

cont. rhy. sim.

spilled some ink on Mom-my's rug, I made Tom-my eat a bug,

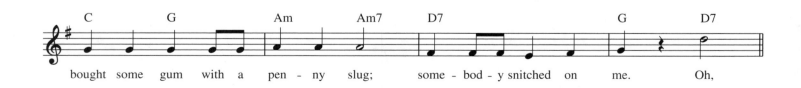

bought some gum with a pen-ny slug; some-bod-y snitched on me. Oh,

Chorus

I'm get-tin' nut-tin' for Christ-mas. Mom-my and

Dad-dy are mad. I'm get-tin' nut-tin' for Christ-mas,

'cause I ain't been nut-tin' but bad. _____ 2. I

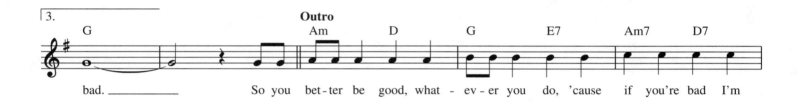

bad. _____ **Outro** So you bet-ter be good, what-ev-er you do, 'cause if you're bad I'm

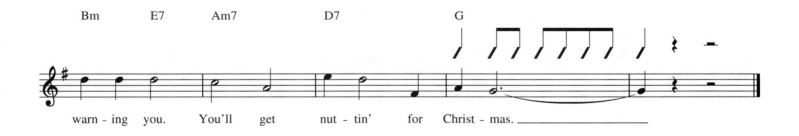

warn-ing you. You'll get nut-tin' for Christ-mas. _____

Additional Lyrics

2. I put a tack on teacher's chair;
Somebody snitched on me.
I tied a knot in Susie's hair;
Somebody snitched on me.
I did a dance on Mommy's plants,
Climbed a tree and tore my pants.
Filled the sugar bowl with ants;
Somebody snitched on me.

3. I won't be seeing Santa Claus;
Somebody snitched on me.
He won't come visit me because
Somebody snitched on me.
Next year, I'll be going straight.
Next year, I'll be good, just wait.
I'd start now but it's too late;
Somebody snitched on me.

O Come, All Ye Faithful
(Adeste Fideles)

Words and Music by John Francis Wade
Latin Words translated by Frederick Oakeley

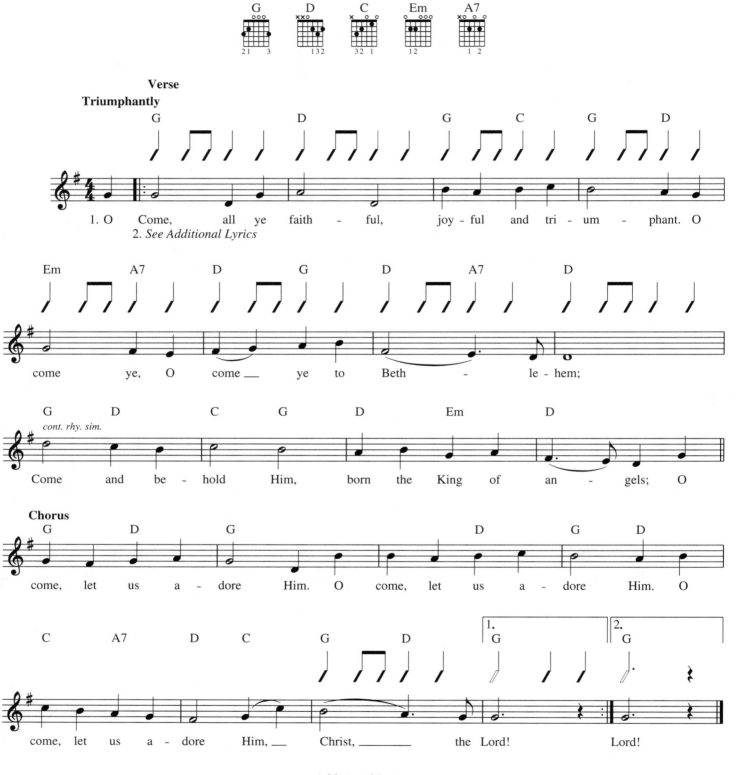

Additional Lyrics

2. Sing choirs of angels, sing in exultation.
   O sing all ye citizens of heaven above.
   Glory to God in the highest.

O Little Town of Bethlehem

Words by Phillips Brooks
Music by Lewis H. Redner

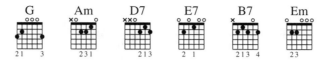

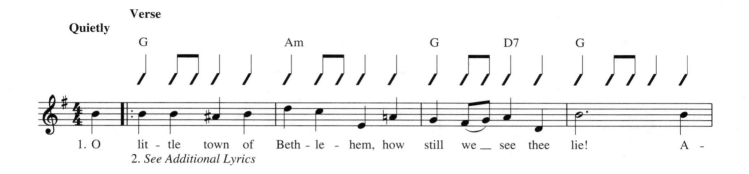

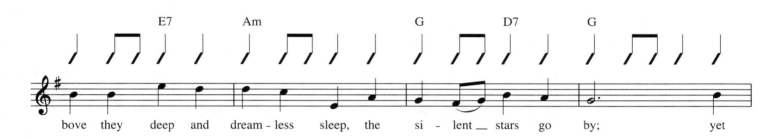

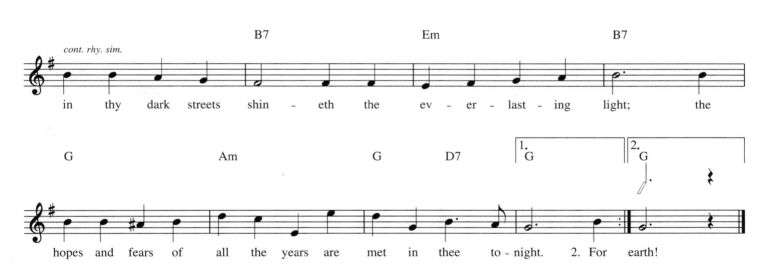

Additional Lyrics

2. For Christ is born of Mary, and gathered all above.
   While mortals sleep the angels keep
   Their watch of wond'ring love.
   O morning stars, together proclaim the holy birth!
   And praises sing to God the King,
   And peace to men on earth!

O Holy Night

English Words by John S. Dwight
Music by Adolphe Adam

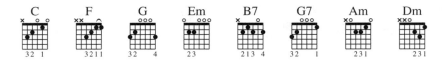

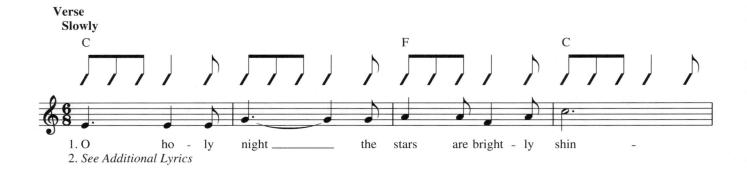

Verse
Slowly

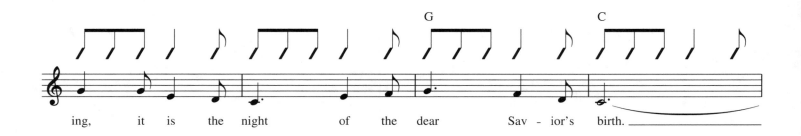

1. O ho-ly night _____ the stars are bright-ly shin -
2. *See Additional Lyrics*

ing, it is the night of the dear Sav-ior's birth. _____

cont. rhy. sim.

_____ Long lay the world _____ in sin and er - ror

pin - ing, 'til he ap - peared and the soul felt its

worth. _____ A thrill of hope the wear - y soul re -

joic - es, for yon - der breaks a new and glor - ious morn.

Chorus

Fall _____ on your knees, _____ oh, hear _____ the an - gel
See Additional Lyrics

voic - es! O night _____ di - vine, _____ O

night _____ when Christ was born! _____ O night! _____ O

ho - ly night! O night di - vine! _____

pow'r _____ and glo - ry _____

ev - er - more pro - claim! _____

Additional Lyrics

2. Truly He taught us to love one another.
His law is love, and His gospel is peace.
Chains shall He break, for the slave is our brother,
And in His name all opression shall cease.
Sweet hymns of joy in grateful chorus raise we.
Let all within us praise His holy name.

Chorus   Christ is the Lord, oh, praise His name forever!
His pow'r and glory evermore proclaim!
His pow'r and glory evermore proclaim!

Old Toy Trains

Words and Music by Roger Miller

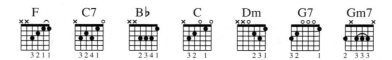

Chorus
Moderately

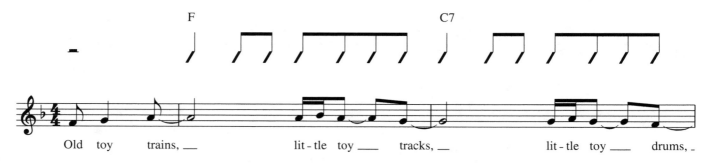

Old toy trains, ___ lit-tle toy ___ tracks, ___ lit-tle toy ___ drums, ___

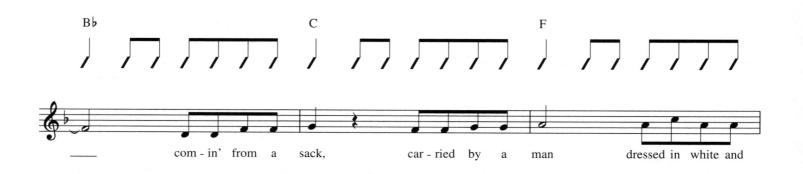

___ com-in' from a sack, car-ried by a man dressed in white and

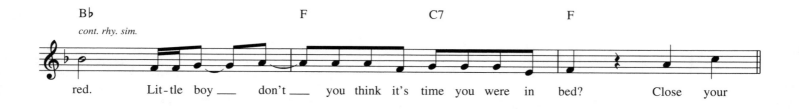

red. Lit-tle boy ___ don't ___ you think it's time you were in bed? Close your

Bridge

eyes, ___ lis-ten to the skies. ___

All is calm, all is well; soon you'll hear Kris

Chorus

Krin - gle and the jin - gle ___ bell bring - in' lit - tle toy ___ trains, ___ lit - tle toy ___ tracks, _

___ lit - tle toy ___ drums ___ com - in' from a sack, car - ried by a

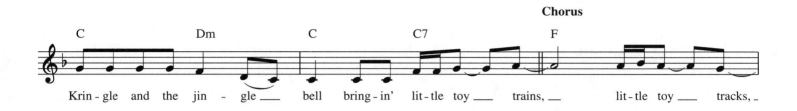

man dressed in white and red. Lit - tle boy ___ don't ___ you think it's time you were in

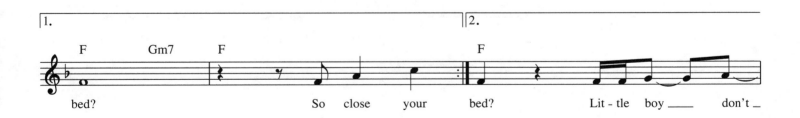

1.

bed? So close your bed?

2.

Lit - tle boy ___ don't _

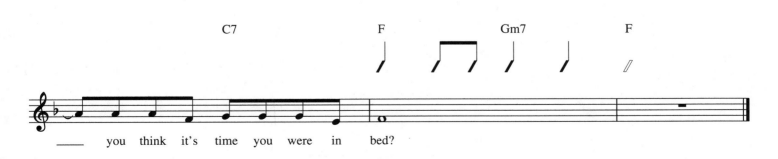

___ you think it's time you were in bed?

One Bright Star

Words and Music by John Jarvis

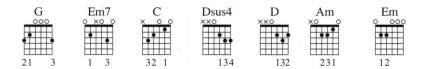

Intro
Moderately slow

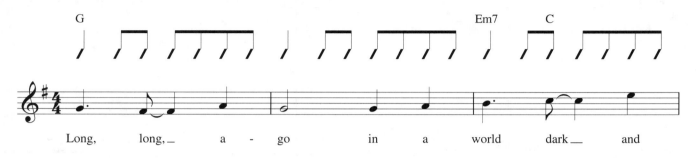

Long, long,_ a - go in a world dark_ and

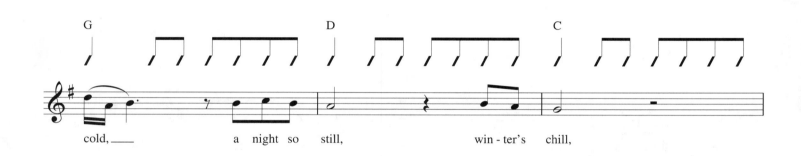

cold,_____ a night so still, win - ter's chill,

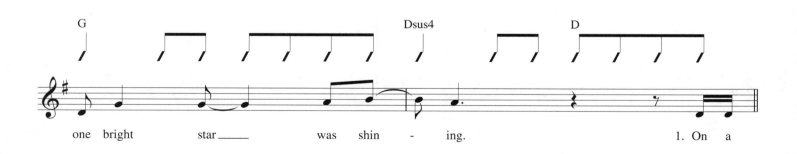

one bright star_____ was shin - ing.

1. On a

Verse

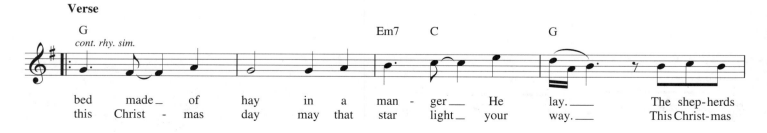

bed made_ of hay in a man - ger_ He lay._ The shep-herds

this Christ - mas day may that star light_ your way._ This Christ-mas

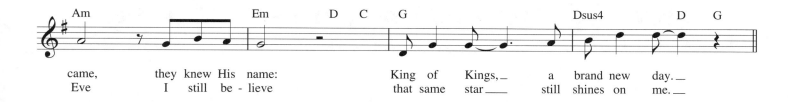

came,   they knew His name: King of Kings,___   a brand new   day.___
Eve   I still be - lieve   that same   star___   still shines on   me.___

Chorus

They ⎱
I   ⎰ saw the light___ in the dark - ness.___   It shines on love___ and

ten - der - ness,___   brings out the hope___ that's in   all___ of us.___   May it

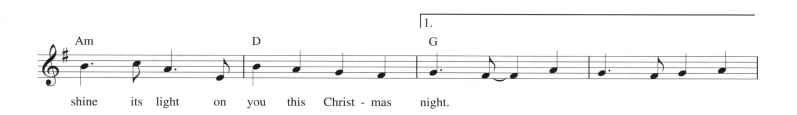

shine   its light   on   you this Christ - mas   night.

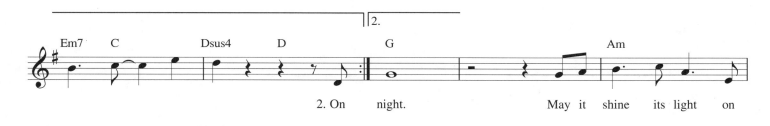

2. On night.   May it shine its light on

Outro

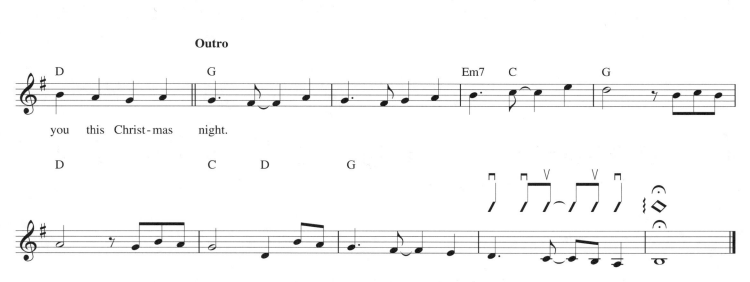

you this Christ - mas   night.

Rockin' Around the Christmas Tree

Music and Lyrics by Johnny Marks

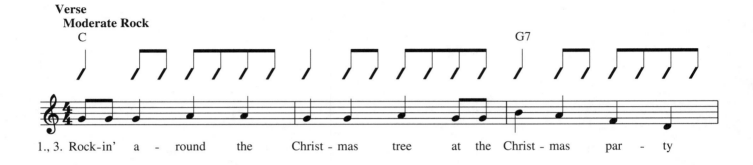

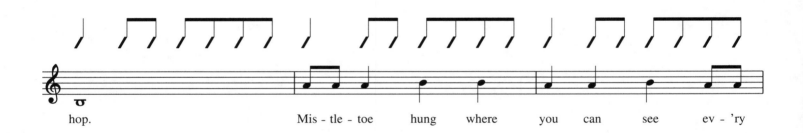

1., 3. Rock-in' a - round the Christ-mas tree at the Christ-mas par - ty

hop. Mis - tle - toe hung where you can see ev - 'ry

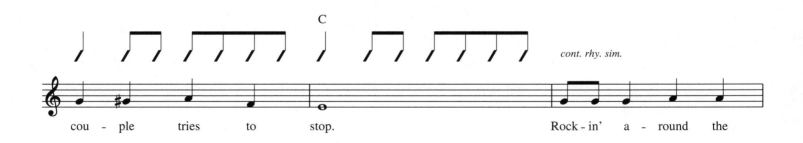

cou - ple tries to stop. Rock-in' a - round the

Christ-mas tree, let the Christ-mas spir - it ring. La - ter we'll have some

pump - kin pie and we'll do some car - ol - ing. You will get a

sen - ti - men - tal feel - ing when you hear voic - es sing - ing,

"Let's be jol - ly. Deck the halls with boughs of hol - ly."

Verse

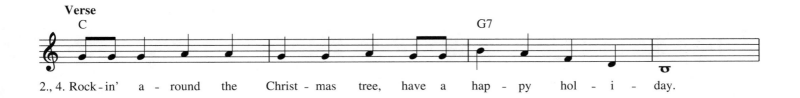

2., 4. Rock - in' a - round the Christ - mas tree, have a hap - py hol - i - day.

1.

Ev - 'ry - one danc - ing mer - ri - ly in the new old fash - ioned way.

2.

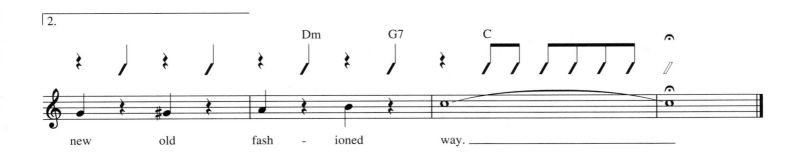

new old fash - ioned way. _____

Rudolph the Red-Nosed Reindeer

Music and Lyrics by Johnny Marks

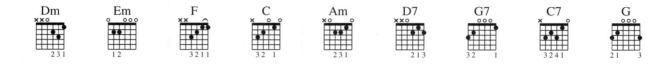

Intro
Rubato

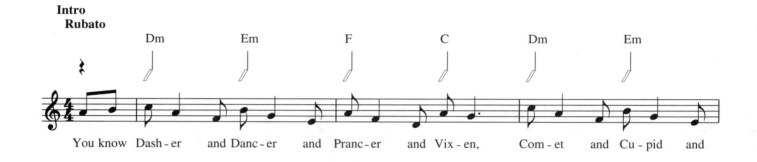

You know Dash-er and Danc-er and Pranc-er and Vix-en, Com-et and Cu-pid and

Don-ner and Blitz-en, but do you re-call the most fa-mous rein-deer of all?

Verse
Lightly

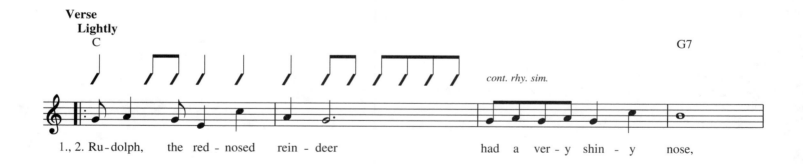

1., 2. Ru-dolph, the red-nosed rein-deer had a ver-y shin-y nose,

and if you ev-er saw it, you would e-ven say it glows.

All of the oth - er rein - deer used to laugh and call him names,

they nev - er let poor Ru - dolph join in an - y rein - deer games.

Bridge

Then one fog - gy Christ - mas Eve, San - ta came to say,

"Ru - dolph, with your nose so bright, won't you guide my sleigh to - night?"

Outro

Then how the rein - deer loved him as they shout - ed out with glee;

"Ru - dolph, the red - nosed rein - deer, you'll go down in his - to - ry!"

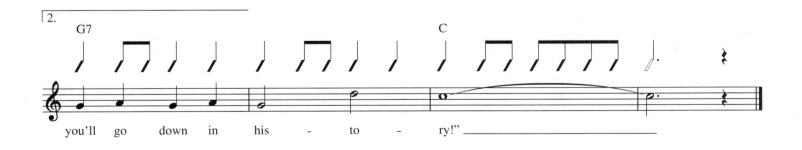

you'll go down in his - to - ry!"

Santa Baby

By Joan Javits, Phil Springer and Tony Springer

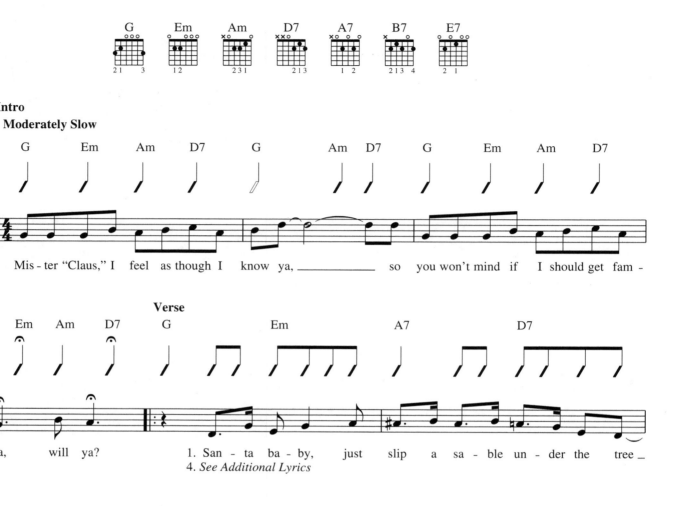

Intro
Moderately Slow

Mis - ter "Claus," I feel as though I know ya, _____ so you won't mind if I should get fam -

Verse

mil - ya, will ya?

1. San - ta ba - by, just slip a sa - ble un - der the tree _____
4. *See Additional Lyrics*

cont. rhy. sim.

_____ for me; _____ been an aw - ful good girl. _____ San - ta ba - by, so

Verse

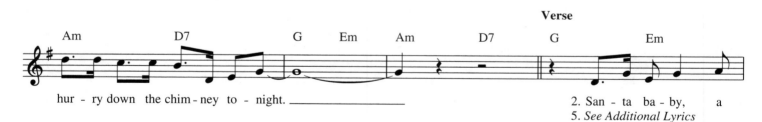

hur - ry down the chim - ney to - night. _____

2. San - ta ba - by, a
5. *See Additional Lyrics*

fif - ty four con - vert - i - ble, too, _____ light blue. _____ I'll wait up for you dear. _____

Santa ba-by, so hur-ry down the chim-ney to-night. _____

Bridge

B7 ... E7

Think of all the fun I've missed. _ Think of all the fel-las that I

See Additional Lyrics

A7 ... D7

have-n't kissed. _ Next year I could be just as good _ if you check off my

Verse

G   Em   A7   D7   G   Em

Christ-mas list.   3. San-ta ba-by,   I want a yacht and real-ly that's not ____ a lot; _

6. *See Additional Lyrics*

A7   D7   G   Em   Am   D7

been an an-gel all year. ____ San-ta ba-by, so hur-ry down the chim-ney to-night. _

1.

G   Em   Am   D7   G   Em   Am   D7   G

2.

Additional Lyrics

4. Santa baby, one little thing I really do need;
   The deed to a platinum mine.
   Santa honey, so hurry down the chimney tonight.

5. Santa cutie and fill my stocking with a duplex and cheques.
   Sign your X on the line.
   Santa cutie, and hurry down the chimney tonight.

Bridge Come and trim my Christmas tree
   With some decorations at Tiffany.
   I really do believe in you.
   Let's see if you believe in me.

6. Santa baby, forgot to mention one little thing, a ring!
   I don't mean on the phone.
   Santa baby, so hurry down the chimney tonight.

Silent Night

Words by Joseph Mohr
Translated by John F. Young
Music by Franz X. Gruber

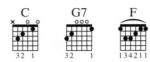

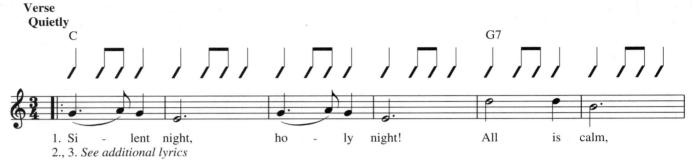

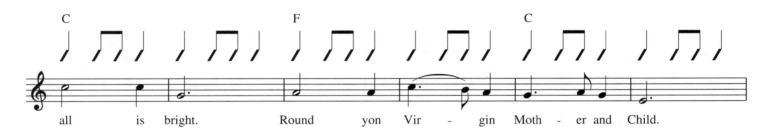

Additional Lyrics

2. Silent night, holy night!
Shepherds quake at the sight.
Glories stream from heaven afar.
Heavenly hosts sing Alleluia.
Christ the Savior is born!
Christ the Savior is born!

3. Silent night, holy night!
Son of God, love's pure light.
Radiant beams from thy holy face
With the dawn of redeeming grace.
Jesus Lord at Thy birth.
Jesus Lord at Thy birth.

Silver and Gold

Music and Lyrics by Johnny Marks

Silver Bells
from the Paramount Picture THE LEMON DROP KID

Words and Music by Jay Livingston and Ray Evans

Additional Lyrics

2. Strings of street lights even stop lights
   Blink a bright red and green,
   As the shoppers rush home with their treasures.
   Hear the snow crunch, see the kids bunch,
   This is Santa's big scene,
   And above all the bustle you hear:

Snowfall

Lyrics by Ruth Thornhill
Music by Claude Thornhill

Intro
Moderately

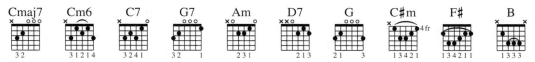

Verse

Play 4 times

1., 4. Snow - fall, _____ soft - ly, _____

mist - y white. Vel - vet breeze 'round my

Verse

door - step. 3., 6. Gent - ly, _____ soft - ly, _____

1.

si - lent _____ snow - fall! _____

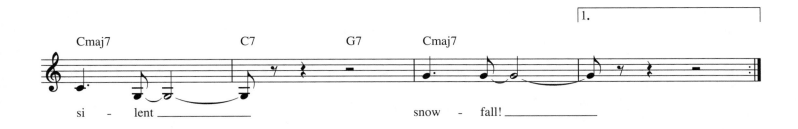

2.

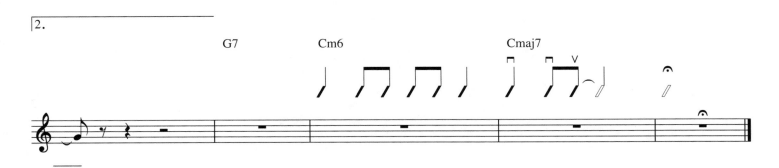

Suzy Snowflake

Words and Music by Sid Tepper and Roy Bennett

Up on the Housetop

Words and Music by B.R. Handy

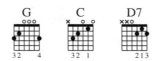

Additional Lyrics

2. First comes the stocking of Little Nell,
Oh, dear Santa, fill it well.
Give her a dollie that laughs and cries,
One that will open and shut her eyes.

This Is Christmas
(Bright, Bright the Holly Berries)

Lyric by Wihla Hutson
Music by Alfred Burt

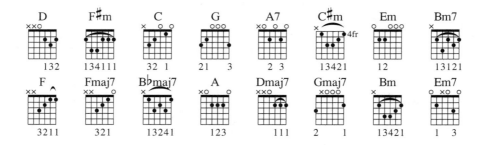

Verse
Liltingly

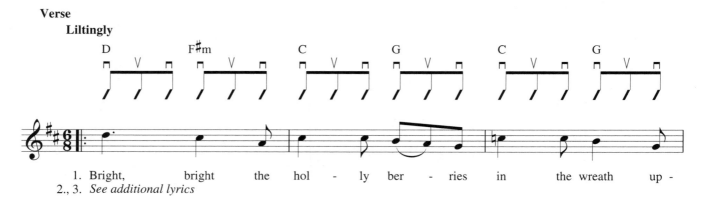

1. Bright, bright the hol - ly ber - ries in the wreath up -
2., 3. *See additional lyrics*

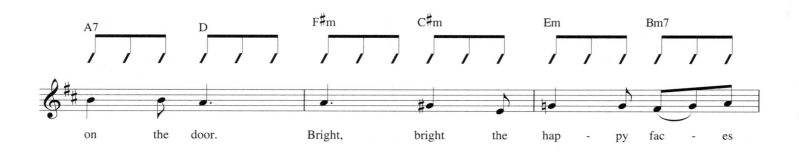

on the door. Bright, bright the hap - py fac - es

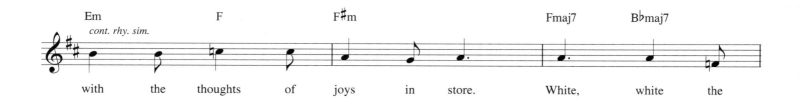

with the thoughts of joys in store. White, white the

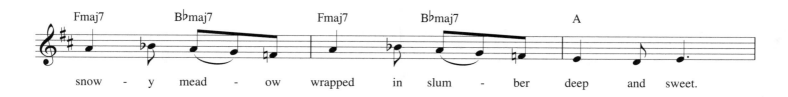

snow - y mead - ow wrapped in slum - ber deep and sweet.

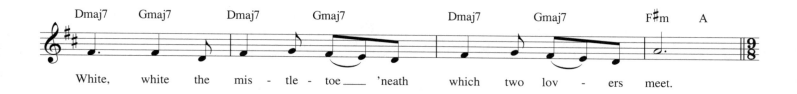

White, white the mis - tle - toe ___ 'neath which two lov - ers meet.

Chorus

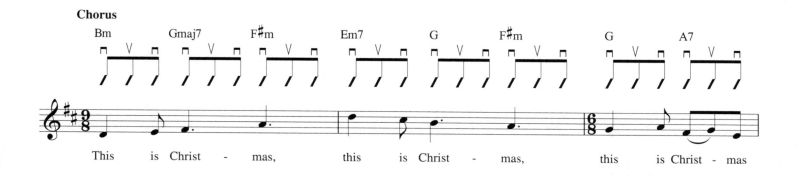

This is Christ - mas, this is Christ - mas, this is Christ - mas

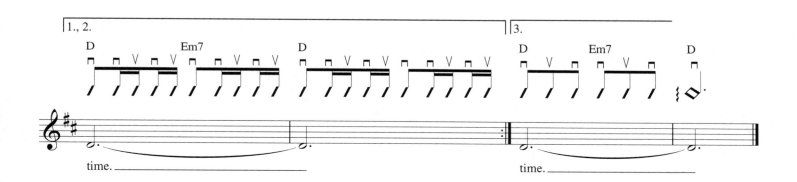

time. _____ time. _____

Additional Lyrics

2. Gay, gay the children's voices filled with laughter, filled with glee.
Gay, gay the tinsled things upon the dark and spicy tree.
Day, day when all mankind may hear the angel's song again.
Day, day when Christ was born to bless the sons of men.

3. Sing, sing ye heav'nly host to tell the blessed Saviour's birth.
Sing, sing in holy joy, ye dwellers all upon the earth.
King, King yet tiny Babe, come down to us from God above.
King, King of ev'ry heart which opens wide to love.

'Twas the Night Before Christmas

Words by Clement Clark Moore
Music by F. Henri Klickman

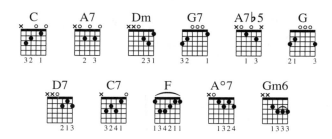

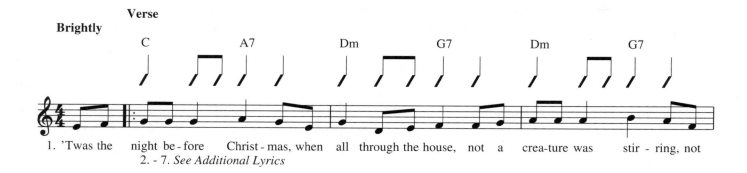

Brightly   **Verse**

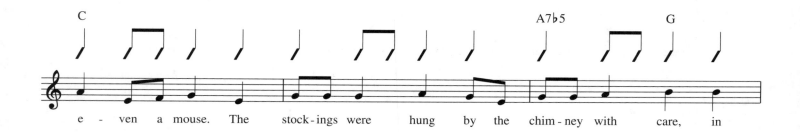

1. 'Twas the night be-fore Christ-mas, when all through the house, not a crea-ture was stir-ring, not
2. - 7. See Additional Lyrics

e - ven a mouse. The stock-ings were hung by the chim-ney with care, in

hopes that Saint Nich-o-las soon would be there. The chil-dren were nest-led all

snug in their beds, while vis-ions of su-gar plums danced through their heads. And

Ma - ma in her 'ker - chief and I in my cap, had just

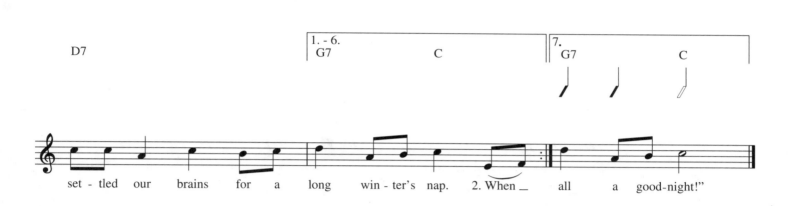

set - tled our brains for a long win - ter's nap. 2. When __ all a good-night!"

Additional Lyrics

2. When out on the lawn there arouse such a clatter;
   I sprang from my bed to see what was the matter.
   Away to the window I flew like a flash,
   Tore open the shutters and threw up the sash.
   The moon, on the breast of the new-fallen snow,
   Gave a lustre of midday to objects below.
   When what to my wondering eyes should appear.
   But a miniature sleigh and eight tiny reindeer.

3. With a little old driver; so lively and quick,
   I knew in a moment it must be Saint Nick.
   More rapid than eagles, his coursers they came
   And he whistled, and shouted, and called them by name;
   "Now, Dasher, Now, Dancer! Now, Prancer! Now, Vixen!
   On Comet! On, Cupid! On Donder and Blitzen!
   To the top of the porch, to the top of the wall!
   Now dash away, dash away, dash away all!"

4. As dry leaves that before the wild hurricane fly,
   When they meet with an obstacle, mount to the sky.
   So up to the house-top the coursers they flew,
   With the sleigh full of toys, and Saint Nicholas, too.
   And then in a twinkling I heard on the roof
   The prancing and pawing of each little hoof.
   As I drew in my head, and was turning around,
   Down the chimney Saint Nicholas came with a bound.

5. He was dressed all in fir from his head to his foot
   And his clothes were all tarnished with ashes and soot.
   And he looked like a peddler just opening his pack.
   His eyes how they twinkled! His dimples how merry!
   His cheeks were like roses, his nose like a cherry,
   His droll little mouth was drawn up like a bow
   And the beard of his chin was as white as the snow.

6. The stump of a pipe he held tight in his teeth
   And the smoke, it encircled his head like a wreath.
   He had a broad face, and a round little belly
   That shook, when he laughed, like a bowl full of jelly.
   He was chubby and plump, a right jolly old elf,
   And I laughed when I saw him, in spite of myself.
   A wink of his eye and a twist of his head,
   Soon gave me to know I had nothing to dread.

7. He spoke not a word but went straight to his work,
   And filled all the stockings, then turned with a jerk,
   And laying his finger aside of his nose,
   And giving a nod, up the chimney he rose.
   He sprang to his sleigh, to his team gave a whistle
   And away they all flew like the down of a thistle,
   But I heard him exclaim, ere he drove out of sight:
   "Happy Christmas to all, and all a good-night!"

The Twelve Days of Christmas

Traditional English Carol

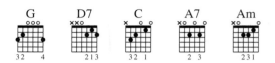

1. On the first day of Christ-mas, my true love gave to me: a par-tridge __ in a pear

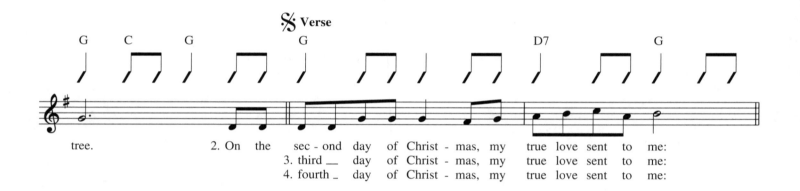

tree. 2. On the sec-ond day of Christ-mas, my true love sent to me:
3. third __ day of Christ-mas, my true love sent to me:
4. fourth __ day of Christ-mas, my true love sent to me:

D.S. for Verses 3. & 4.

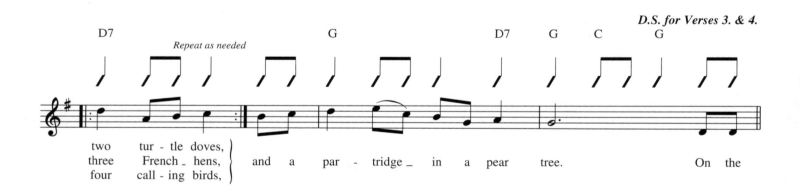

two tur-tle doves,
three French __ hens, and a par-tridge __ in a pear tree. On the
four call-ing birds,

5. fifth day of Christ-mas, my true love sent to me: five gold _____

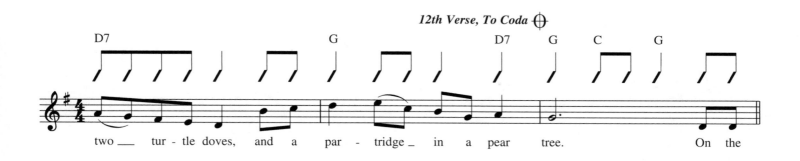

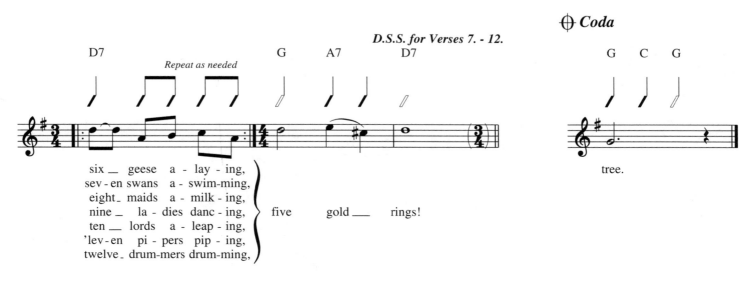

We Need a Little Christmas

from MAME

Music and Lyric by Jerry Herman

Verse
Brightly

1. Haul out the hol - ly. _____ Put up the
2. *See Additional Lyrics*

tree be - fore my spir - it falls _____ a - gain.

cont. rhy. sim.

Fill up the stock - ing. _____ I may be

rush - ing things, but deck the halls _____ a - gain

now. _____

For we
3. For we

need a lit - tle Christ - mas, right this ver - y min - ute,
need a lit - tle mu - sic, need a lit - tle laugh - ter,

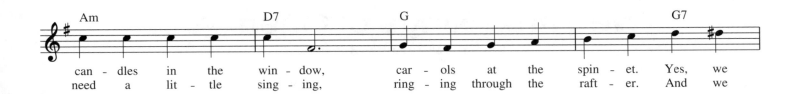

can - dles   in   the   win - dow,   car - ols   at   the   spin - et.   Yes, we
need   a   lit - tle   sing - ing,   ring - ing through the   raft - er.   And we

1.

To Coda ⊕

need   a   lit - tle   Christ - mas,   right   this   ver - y   min - ute.   It
need   a   lit - tle   snap - py   "hap - py   ev - er

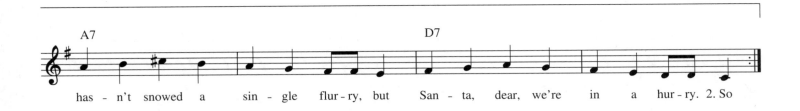

has - n't snowed   a   sin - gle   flur - ry, but   San - ta,   dear, we're   in   a   hur - ry. 2. So

2.   *D.S. al Coda*

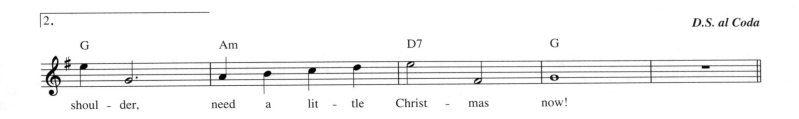

shoul - der,   need   a   lit - tle   Christ - mas   now!

⊕ *Coda*

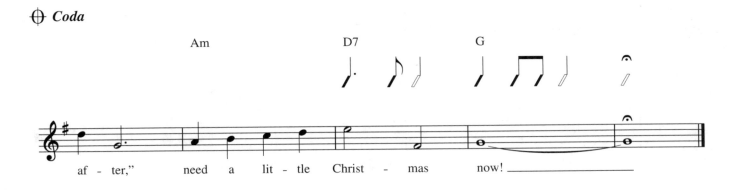

af - ter,"   need   a   lit - tle   Christ - mas   now! _____

Additional Lyrics

2. So climb down the chimney,
   Turn on the brightest string of lights I've ever seen.
   Slice up the fruitcake.
   It's time we hung some tinsel on the evergreen bough.
   For I've grown a little leaner, grown a little colder,
   Grown a little sadder, grown a little older,
   And I need a little angel, sitting on my shoulder,
   Need a little Christmas now!

We Three Kings of Orient Are

Words and Music by John H. Hopkins

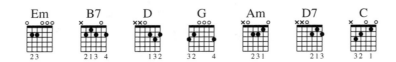

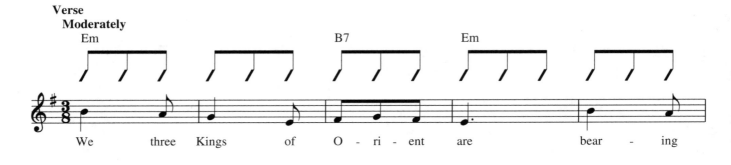

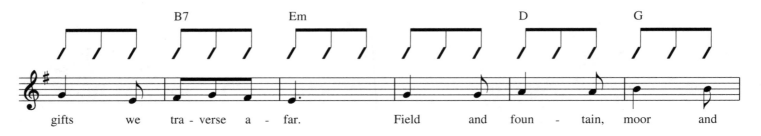

Verse
Moderately

We three Kings of O - ri - ent are bear - ing

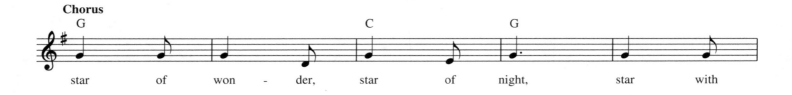

gifts we tra - verse a - far. Field and foun - tain, moor and

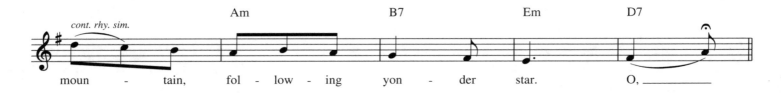

moun - tain, fol - low - ing yon - der star. O,

Chorus

star of won - der, star of night, star with

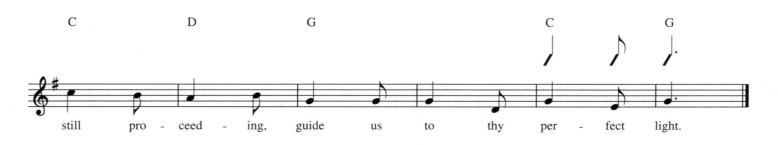

roy - al beau - ty bright. West - ward lead - ing,

still pro - ceed - ing, guide us to thy per - fect light.

We Wish You a Merry Christmas

Traditional English Folksong

Additional Lyrics

2. We all know that Santa's coming.
We all know that Santa's coming.
We all know that Santa's coming
And soon will be here.

What Are You Doing New Year's Eve?

By Frank Loesser

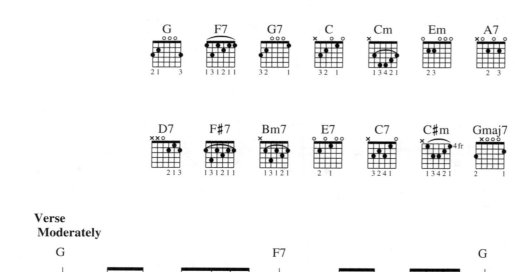

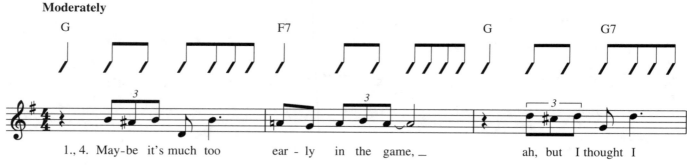

Verse
Moderately

1., 4. May-be it's much too ear - ly in the game, __ ah, but I thought I

ask you just the same, __ what are you do - ing new year's, New Year's

Verse

Eve?   2., 5. Won - der whose arms will hold you good and tight, __

cont. rhy. sim.

when it's ex - act - ly twelve o' - clock that night, __ wel - com-ing in the

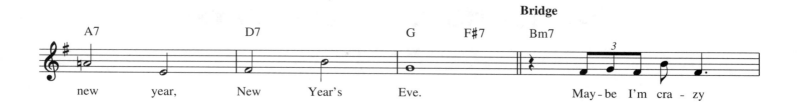

Bridge

new year, New Year's Eve. May-be I'm cra-zy

to sup - pose I'd ev - er be the one you chose

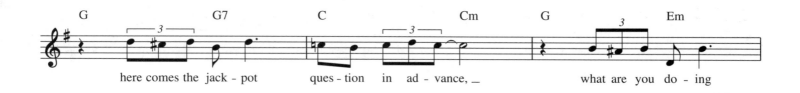

out of the thou - sand in - vi - ta - tions you'll re -

Verse

ceive. 3., 6. Ah, but in case I stand one lit - tle chance, __

here comes the jack - pot ques - tion in ad - vance, __ what are you do - ing

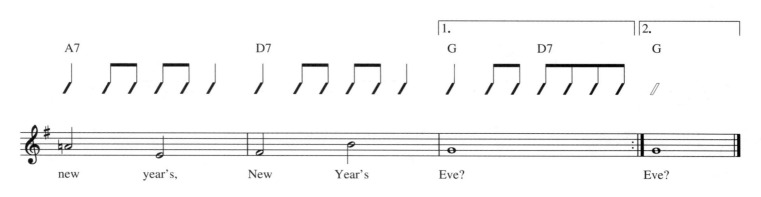

new year's, New Year's Eve? Eve?

Wonderful Christmastime

Words and Music by McCartney

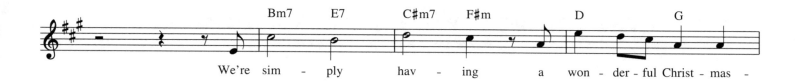

We're sim - ply hav - ing a won - der - ful Christ - mas -

D.C. al Coda
(take 2nd ending)

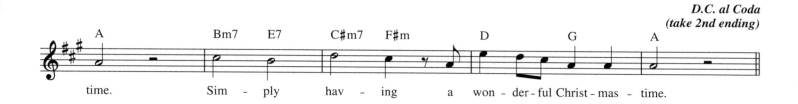

time. Sim - ply hav - ing a won - der - ful Christ - mas - time.

Coda

Ding dong, ding dong, ding dong, ding dong, ding dong, ding

dong, dong dong, dong, dong. The par - ty's on, ___ the spir - it's up, _

___ we're here to - night _ and that's e - nough. _

Outro-Chorus

Repeat & Fade

Sim - ply hav - ing a won - der - ful Christ - mas - time. We're

Additional Lyrics

2. The party's on,
   The feeling's here
   That only comes
   This time of year.

3. The word is out
   About the town,
   To lift a glass.
   Oh, don't look down.

You Make It Feel Like Christmas

Words and Music by Neil Diamond

Intro

Moderately slow Rock

Co-zy we are, clos-er than far, sounds of for-ev-er still

a-round.
1. Lov-ers in love, just like we were 'cause
2. Look at the sun shin-ing on me; look at us now, part of it all. In

be-in' a-part's a lone-ly sound. And when peo-ple ask how
no-where could be a bet-ter place. Lov-ers in love, yeah,
spite of it all, we're still a-round. So wake up the kids, and

we stay to-geth-er, I say you nev-er let me down. Yeah,
that's what we'll be. When you're here with me, it's Christ-mas Day. 'Cause
put on some tea. Let's light up the tree; it's Christ-mas Day. And

Chorus

you make it feel ___ like Christ - mas   e - ven when things _ go   wrong. _

___   I hear the sound _ of Christ - mas   in your song _

___   all   year   long.

1.   2.

That's how you know that it's true, ba - by.

3.

3. Just   Yes, you know I do babe,

all   year   long. _____

You're Not Alone

Words and Music by Shawn Stockman

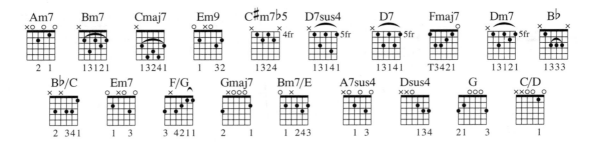

Tune down ½ step:
(low to high) E♭ - A♭ - D♭ - G♭ - B♭ - E♭

Intro
Moderately slow

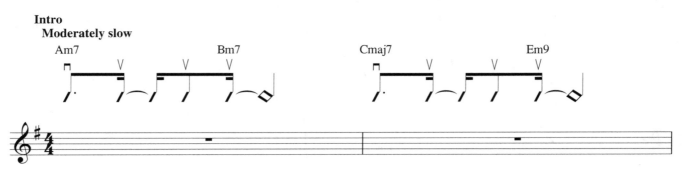

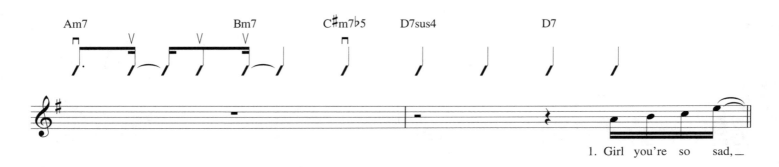

1. Girl you're so sad,___

Verse

_____ he was the ver - y first love___ you had_____ but he hurt___ your heart___ real bad.___
2., 3., 4. *See additional lyrics*

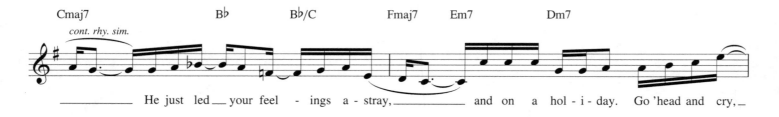

_____ He just led___ your feel - ings a - stray,_____ and on a hol - i - day. Go 'head and cry,___

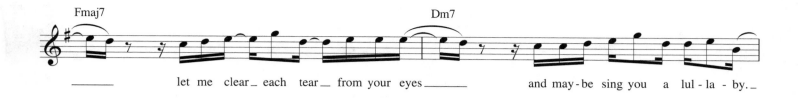

let me clear___ each tear___ from your eyes_____ and may-be sing you a lul - la - by._

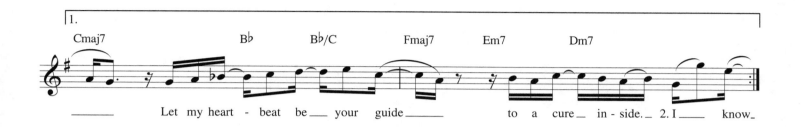

1.

Cmaj7   B♭   B♭/C   Fmaj7   Em7   Dm7

_____ Let my heart - beat be___ your guide_____ to a cure___ in - side.___ 2. I___ know_

2.

Cmaj7   B♭   F/G

gain. I___ can be___ the___ key___ for your heart___ to mend. 'Cause ba - by you're not a - lone.___

Chorus

Cmaj7   Gmaj7

_____ The pain___ in your heart___ is___ strong.___ Ba - by let___ me___ hold you in my arms.___

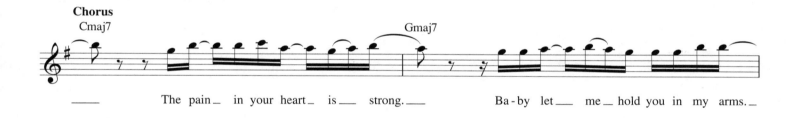

Cmaj7   Bm7/E

_____ Let me be___ your pro-tec - tor from harm.___ 'Cause no___ one should be___ a - lone___

To Coda ⊕

A7sus4   Dsus4   G   Em7

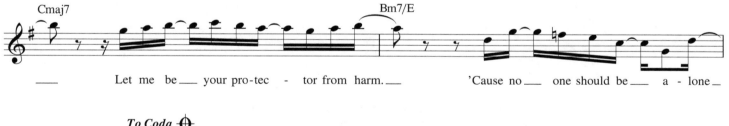

_____ on Christ - mas. _____

D.S. al Coda
(take repeat)

⊕ **Coda**

Cmaj7   Bm7   G   C/D

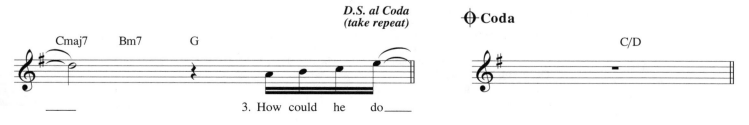

_____ 3. How could he do___

Interlude

Spoken: Girl, this Christmas you won't be alone, you don't have to cry, you don't have to worry about a thing.
Don't live in the past, baby, I'm your future. All the feelings that I have are for you. And anything that I can do to take away any problem that you

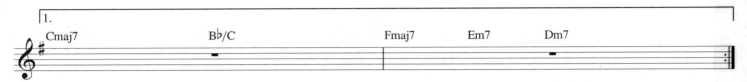

1.

All the gifts that you wanted this year are yours.   You dont have to worry 'bout him no more 'cause he's gone.

2.

may have or have had, I'm here. Just say, "Michael" and this Christmas is yours.

'Cause ba - by you're not   a - lone. __

Outro-Chorus

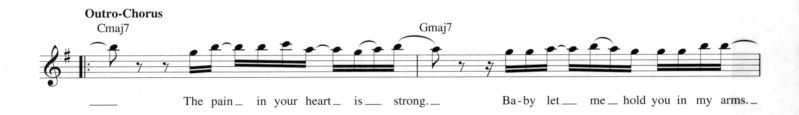

__   The pain __ in your heart __ is __ strong. __   Ba-by let __ me __ hold you in my arms. __

Repeat and fade

__   Let me be __ your pro - tec   -   tor from harm, __   'cause no __ one should be _____ a - lone. __

Additional Lyrics

2. I know that it's, oh, so hard to let go.
   Give yourself time to heal, take it, slow.
   Let's talk as the rainbow colored lights make the tree glow.
   I'm your friend, I will be here for you 'til the end
   'Cause I don't wanna see you hurt again.
   I can be the key for your heart to mend.

3. How could he do such a thing to one as good as you?
   Gave him your all and I know that it's true.
   Had a gem and didn't know what to do.
   But baby I'm here to tell you that I'm yours if you want me.
   These feelings I've held in too long. You've been on my mind.
   Girl, you know I'll never find love that's so kind.

4. I open up to pray that by the Lord's grace you would come my
   Way and receive love that won't go away.
   Celebrate this occasion with gifts of joy on His birthday.
   On this night, I'll fill all your empty spaces inside.
   Hold you close and make ev'rything alright,
   'Cause this day is for sharing and no one should be without someone caring.